BATHROOM BOOK

of

MICHIGAN TRIVIA

Weird, Wacky and Wild

Brian Hudson & Andrew Fleming
Illustrations by Patrick Hénaff &
Roger Garcia

BLUE
BIKE
BOOKS

The Publisher: Blue Bike Books
www.bluebikebooks.com

Library and Archives Canada Cataloguing in Publication

Hudson, Brian, 1975–
    Bathroom book of Michigan trivia / Brian Hudson and Andrew Fleming.

ISBN-13: 978-1-897278-32-1
ISBN-10: 1-897278-32-2

    1. Michigan—Miscellanea. I. Fleming, Andrew, 1972– II. Title.

F566.6.H83 2007   977.4   C2007-903202-8

Project Director: Nicholle Carrière
Project Editor: Wendy Pirk
Proofreader: Ashley Johnson
Production: Alexander Penrose
Illustrations: Patrick Hénaff, Roger Garcia, Peter Tyler, Roly Wood

We acknowledge the support of the Alberta Foundation for the Arts for our publishing program.

Alberta
Foundation
for the Arts

PC: P5

DEDICATION

This one's for my parents, who made me a Michigander.

−BPH

ACKNOWLEDGMENTS

The biggest thanks go out to my wonderful wife Robin, without whom this book wouldn't have been written; she is my rock in everything I do. I would also like to thank my publisher, for giving me this chance, and editors Wendy Pirk and Ashley Johnson, for all their hard work.

−BPH

I would like to thank the Detroit border guard who, after great and lengthy deliberation, finally decided I was worthy of entering the great state of Michigan. And also to Iggy Pop, Eminem and the White Stripes for providing the background music this book was mostly written to.

−Andrew

CONTENTS

INTRODUCTION

My parents were transient Michiganders. They came to the state from New York (like so many New Yorkers before them) and have since left for warmer climates. But in their time here, they made me a life-long Michigander, born and raised. So when the opportunity came up to write this book, I went for it.

I've lived most of my life in the Detroit area, like so many Michiganders do, and as a child I had no special love for the state. It wasn't until college, when I ventured out of Detroit and into the more northern and western portions of the state, that I began to appreciate just what kind of place Michigan is. Its stunning array of peoples, traditions and history make it a truly singular place. Writing this book has only served to broaden my appreciation of the state I call home. I hope that reading it will open your eyes to the state's quirks and treasures, too, whether you are just visiting or are a Michigander like me.

−BPH

WHAT SETS MICHIGAN APART

Michigan is a state of incredible variety. While most out-of-staters know Michigan for its Detroit flavor (cars, guns and Motown), the truth is that there's a whole state full of people, places and local traditions, a fantastic array of diversity and interest. Everyone can find something to enjoy in Michigan. Consider the land. Our diversity of weather, water and soil lets us grow a wealth of crops, allowing us to be a leading producer of apples, cherries, beans and potatoes. That same land can provide for an unlimited amount of fun. With water, beaches, rivers, forests, dunes, mountains and islands, Michigan offers every imaginable outdoor sport and activity. Visit any wooded area in Michigan, and chances are you can fish there in spring, hike there in summer, hunt there in autumn and ski or snowmobile through the area in winter. All without traveling far!

Michigan also has a melting pot heritage that may rival New York City. Waves of immigrants from across Europe and Asia have lent Michigan a unique diversity. From the Cornish and Finnish influence of the Upper Peninsula to the Dutch-inspired beauty of Holland and the ethnic pockets of Detroit and its suburbs, the state has always welcomed new arrivals with open arms (or maybe an open mitten). This diversity has given the state a profound respect for all cultures that come here. It's no wonder that Michigan became a stronghold of the Civil Rights movement.

Today, Michigan is faced with a changing world economy and a fundamental shift in the nature of its industry. But even in these difficult times, its unique variety assures that Michigan will remain a standout amongst America's fifty states.

ANIMALS OF THE STATE

State Animal

There aren't many wolverines left in "The Wolverine State." Not a single one had been spotted in two hundred years until a confirmed sighting in February 2004 near the town of Ubly. The wolverine (*Gulo gulo*), also known commonly as the glutton or carcajou, is the largest land-dwelling member of the weasel family and is considered to be, pound for pound, the most ferocious animal on earth. Resembling a small bear that works out a lot, the wolverine generally weighs only between 25 to 65 pounds (the male is around 30 percent larger than the female) but has been known to kill prey as large as a moose. The wolverine has glossy brown fur with stripes of yellow along the sides and a long tail. Its fur is very dense and frost-resistant.

 The University of Michigan's varsity sports teams are all named the Wolverines, and Detroit had a major league baseball team in the 19th century by the same name. There is a village named Wolverine in Cheboygan County, a Wolverine Lake in Oakland County, and a passenger train called the Wolverine operating between Pontiac and Chicago.

State Game Animal
The white-tailed deer (*Odocoileus virginianus*) is found in every county in Michigan. Also known as the Virginia deer, the white-tailed is named for the characteristic white underside of its tail, which shows like a white flag of surrender when the deer flees. The male (buck) usually weighs 130 to 220 pounds and the female (doe) 90 to 130 pounds. The coat is a reddish brown in spring and summer and turns to a grayish brown for the rest of the year. A male five years or older has antlers that he uses as a weapon during mating season and then sheds. The white-tailed deer is also the state animal of Arkansas, Illinois, Mississippi, New Hampshire, Ohio, Pennsylvania, Michigan, South Carolina and Wisconsin, as well as the provincial animal of Saskatchewan.

Happiness is a Warm Gun
Killing deer is a popular pastime in Michigan, and citizens are allowed to start hunting deer with a bow and arrow at the age of 10, and with a firearm at age 12. In a somewhat quixotic twist, it is legal to leave food out for deer but is illegal to bait them with food. In 2006, an estimated 258,000 deer were killed—about one deer for every 40 residents.

 A French journalist once asked Michigan rock star and noted hunting enthusiast Ted Nugent: "What do you think the last thought is in the head of a deer before you shoot it?" "They aren't capable of that kind of thinking," the Nuge replied. "All they care about is: 'What am I going to eat next?', 'Who am I going to screw next?' and 'Can I run fast enough to get away?' They are very much like the French."

State Fish

The eastern brook trout, a member of the salmon family, shares the distinction of also being the official fish of New Jersey, New York, Pennsylvania and West Virginia. Commonly known as the speckled trout, the brook trout (*Salvelinus fontinalis*) is usually between 10 and 20 inches long, weighs 3 to 4 pounds, and is known for providing fishermen with a fairly decent fight for its size. Apart from humans, only sea lampreys prey on it. The brook trout itself prefers insects, crayfish, leeches and, of course, smaller fish. It matures at age three and spawns in streams. The male grows a huge, hooked lower jaw called a "kype" and turns a bright color as it dies. The brook trout is restocked in Michigan each year to help keep its numbers up.

 Since 1933, the Lower Peninsula town of Kalkaska has hosted the annual National Trout Festival, a large-scale celebration of all things trout. Kalkaska, immortalized by visiting author and fisherman Ernest Hemingway in the short stories "The Light of the World" and "The Battler," is also home to the National Trout Memorial, a fountain featuring an 18-foot-long brook trout as its centerpiece.

State Bird

Michigan's official bird is famous for rocking in the treetops all day long, hopping and a-bopping and a-singing its song. A migratory songbird in the thrush family, the American robin

(*Turdus migratorius*) is also the state bird of both Connecticut and Wisconsin and has a range from Alaska to Newfoundland and Florida. The robin is around 10 inches long and is distinguished by its brick-red breast. The male's breast is generally brighter than that of the female, and during the breeding season, the male grows temporary, eye-catching black feathers on its head to help attract females. The robin is also noteworthy for producing eggs that inspired the name for a distinct shade of blue.

There has been a fair bit of discussion about changing the state bird status to the tufted titmouse, a bird that, unlike the robin (which has the good sense to leave during the winter) lives in Michigan year-round. Alternatively, some Michiganders believe that male geese—or, more specifically, the gander—would make for an even more apt choice.

DID YOU  KNOW?

Michigan's state animal and state bird both have comic book superheroes named after them. The clawed, indestructible X-Man known as Wolverine is one of Marvel Comics' most popular characters, while the red-vested Robin is, of course, Batman's faithful teenaged sidekick.

State Reptile

Michigan's official cold-blooded critter is the painted turtle (*Chrysemys picta*), a type of turtle found from northern Mexico to southern Canada. It is named for its beautiful shell, which features red markings at the margins so intricate they seem painted on, and it lives in ponds, lakes, marshes and in slow-moving rivers that have soft muddy bottoms. During cold weather, of which Michigan has plenty, the painted turtle hibernates, burying itself for months in the mud beneath streams and ponds. The mud acts as an insulator and helps to keep the turtle from freezing. The painted turtle can survive long winters in ice-covered ponds because they can live for several months without breathing oxygen.

Turtles have powerful symbolic value to the Native American tribes of the Great Lakes. One legend details how the turtle's back provided a base for the first land that was formed in the midst of the great waters. Mackinac Island takes its name from a word in the Ottawa language meaning "great turtle."

DID YOU KNOW?

Weather temperatures determine the sex of painted turtles. In the early summer, females bury their eggs in soft, sandy soil that has good exposure to the sun. Low temperatures during the incubation period produce males while higher temperatures produce females. Incubation usually takes 70 to 80 days, but hatchlings will often spend the entire winter in the nest and only emerge the following spring.

MORE STATE SYMBOLS

State Flower

It was first adopted in 1897 and made official a century later; Michigan's state flower is the apple blossom. Apples are big business in Michigan—they're the state's number one fruit crop and contribute $400–500 million to the annual economy. There are over eight million apple trees in commercial production on over 1000 farms, most of which are family run and have less than 100 acres of orchards each. The most common apple varieties grown are the Red Delicious, the Golden Delicious and the up-and-coming Royal Gala.

DID YOU KNOW?

The minimalist Michigan-born musical duo known as the White Stripes came out with a song titled "Apple Blossom" on their 2000 sophomore album, *De Stilj*. Although the song has nothing to do with the Grammy-winners' home state, the McCartney-esque ditty is notable for marking the first recording of Jack White playing the piano.

State Wildflower

In 1997, there was a coup in Michigan's state flower department. The previous year, the Michigan Wildflower Association held an informal wildflower preference poll in newspapers statewide. Voters were asked to nominate one of six native flowers to be the official flower, and the white trillium (*Trillium grandiflorum*) claimed the honor, taking the dwarf lake iris (*Iris lacustris*) down 1733 to 1479. However, while the white trillium grows throughout eastern North America, the dwarf lake iris blooms only in the Great Lakes area, mostly in Michigan, and is listed as an endangered species. State lawmakers swapped flowers accordingly and declared the dwarf lake iris the new champion. The Michigan Wildflower Association was incensed by the move, calling it "an outrageous power play by select environmental interests over the interests of the people of Michigan."

State Tree

Michigan's state tree, the eastern white pine *(Pinus strobus)*, is the tallest tree east of the Rockies. Untouched old-growth forests nearly 500 years old still remain in the Upper Peninsula's Huron Mountains and the Lower Peninsula's Hartwick Pines State Park and Menomonie Indian Reservation. Eastern white pine ranges from Minnesota to Newfoundland and south along the Appalachian Mountains to Georgia. During the Age of Sail, the tall trees, with their high quality wood, were prized for making sturdy masts.

Pine Enshrined

The eastern white pine is also the state tree of Maine (and its pine cones are Maine's rather unorthodox "state flower"), the provincial tree of Ontario, and the Tree of Great Peace of the Iroquois Nation, a union of several tribes of northeastern Native Americans.

DID YOU KNOW?

By weight, white pine needles contain five times the amount of vitamin C found in lemons, and they make an excellent tea.

State Soil

Kalkaska Sand was first described in 1927 and was one of the first soil series to be recognized in Michigan. Kalkaska covers nearly a million acres in 33 of the state's 83 counties and is found in both the Upper and Lower peninsulas. This multicolored soil is nicknamed "lion's mane" because it is dark at the surface and gets lighter the deeper you dig. The surface layer is black to dark brown, middle layers are dark reddish brown and the subsoil is a sandy, yellowish brown. The soils formed after the glaciers retreated from the area, and they naturally support hardwood timber, yellow birch and sugar maple in particular. Kalkaska is also used to grow Christmas trees and other specialty crops such as strawberries and potatoes.

State Stone

Petoskey stone (*Hexagonaria pericarnata*) is composed of fossilized coral skeletons from 350 million years ago, when Michigan was covered with a shallow sea. Glaciers that covered the state about two million years ago plucked the stones and scattered them over the Lower Peninsula. When dry, the stone resembles ordinary limestone, but when wet or polished, the distinctive mottled pattern of the fossil emerges. Most of the Petoskey stones found along beaches and in gravel have already been rounded and smoothed by glacial and water action.

DID YOU KNOW?

Petoskey stones get their name from an Ottawa Chief named Petosegay, said to be the descendant of French nobleman and fur trader Atoinne Carre, and whose own name meant "rising sun" or "rays of dawn." The city of Petoskey, near where most of the stones have been found, is also named in his honor.

State Fossil

The long-extinct mammal known as the mastodon was named Michigan's main fossil in 2002, thanks to the efforts of students at Ann Arbor's Slauson Middle School, who petitioned on the furry, elephant-like beast's behalf after the remains of the world's longest mastodon trail was discovered nearby. Casts of the 30 footprints are now displayed at the University of Michigan's Museum of Natural History, also home to a completely reconstructed female mastodon skeleton. Mastodons spread over a wide range of North America but were particularly found in the spruce forests of the Eastern U.S. and Michigan's Lower Peninsula; over 250 piles of their remains have been found in the area.

The Elephant Clan

Often confused with wooly mammoths, American mastodons *(Mammut americanum)* were similar in height, at roughly 10 feet at the shoulder, but were stockier, with wider heads and smaller teeth more suited to chewing leaves than grazing trees. The name mastodon was given for its prominent mastoid teeth.

DID YOU KNOW?

Mastodons first appeared on the scene about four million years ago and died out only 10,000 years ago. They were an important food source for prehistoric humans, and experts are still trying to determine what role, if any, our ancestors played in causing their extinction.

State Mineral

Unlike most other states, Michigan has yet to declare an official mineral. Many Michiganders think road salt, mostly made of sodium and chloride, would make for an ideal candidate seeing as how the state would pretty much grind to a halt during the long winters if roads weren't regularly sprinkled with it.

State Gem

Isle Royale greenstone, a variety of pumpellyite, is a mineral named for Isle Royale, the island in Lake Superior where it was first discovered in 1847. Declared the official state gem in 1972, Isle Royale greenstone is also known as chlorastrolite, literally "green star stone," and occurs as amygdules, or cavity fillings, in certain lava flows found only on the island and nearby Keweenaw peninsula.

The Tortoise and the Cat

Greenstone specimens are usually quite small. When dug or naturally weathered out of the lava, they are, unsurprisingly, greenish in color. When polished, either naturally by waves and sand or artificially, they generally exhibit a distinctive mosaic pattern referred to as "turtleback" and are also usually "chatoyant"— meaning they have a gleam resembling a cat's eye.

Many of the old rock tailings from the mining era have greenstones in them. Interested gem hunters should look for the dark green nodules in the rocks they find. Sometimes the greenstones will have weathered out of the rock and can be found lying on the ground. The problem, of course, is getting them out of the rock without damaging them, and only a small percentage of all greenstones found will be gem quality.

WHAT'S IN A NAME?

State Motto

Si quaeris peninsulam amoenam circumspice—"If you seek a pleasant peninsula, look about you." The state motto was taken from the words of a famous British architect who died over a century before Michigan joined the Union and, needless to say, never laid eyes on the place. Sir Christopher Michael Wren, the designer of over 50 churches, including St. Paul's Cathedral, was instead describing his influence on rebuilding London after the Great Fire of 1666.

Unofficial mottos include "Michigan: first line of defense from the Canadians," "At least we're not Wisconsin" and "If you seek a pleasant isthmus, or perhaps even a pleasant cape, we've got those too."

State Name

It is generally accepted that the state was named for Lake Michigan. The word itself is a "Frenchified" take on the Chippewa word *misshikama*, meaning "big lake." Another possibility is that the name comes from the Chippewa word *majigan*, meaning "a clearing." In any case, Michigan has a lot of clearings and lakes.

The Wolverine State

As mentioned earlier, wolverines aren't commonly found in Michigan and, according to the Michigan Historical Center, probably never were. There are a few theories as to how the state earned the nickname the Wolverine State, which was first recorded in an 1846 issue of *Knickerbocker Magazine*. One of the more charitable theories suggests that the name arose because the fur trade was a vital part of the state's early history, and dense, frost-resistant wolverine pelts were highly prized by northern explorers. Wolverines are also commonly known as gluttons, which is a literal translation of their Latin genus name *Gulo,* and the nickname might have been given to early Michiganders for their vicious and greedy actions, either by Native Americans, who saw their land stolen from them, or by Ohioans, from an 1835 dispute over the Ohio–Michigan border known as the Toledo War.

The Automotive State

Michigan essentially gave the world wheels as the very first mass-produced cars rolled out of its factories. America's three major auto manufacturers—General Motors, Ford and Chrysler—all began in Michigan during the early twentieth century and dominated the global industry for decades until the Japanese and others figured out how to build better cars more cheaply.

The Great Lakes State

Michigan shores border four of the five Great Lakes—Superior, Huron, Erie and Michigan—and also Lake St. Clair, which aspires to greatness. Michigan also has over 11,000 inland lakes. When in Michigan, you are never more than six miles from an inland lake or over 85 miles from one of the Great Lakes.

State Song

Not many people know the words to Michigan's official state song. Written by Giles Kavanagh and H. O'Reilly Clint in 1933, "My Michigan" was named an official, but not the official song, by the Legislature five years later. The song has rarely been heard since—the lyrics are still under copyright protection, and the only copies of the sheet music are stashed in the Rare Book Room of the Library of Michigan and the Bentley Historical Library at the University of Michigan.

No, MY Michigan!

Most Michiganders are far more familiar with the similarly titled "Michigan, My Michigan," which has been sung since the days of the Civil War. Winifred Lee Brent Lyster of Detroit wrote the lyrics for the first version in 1862 after stealing the melody from "O Tannenbaum" ("O Christmas Tree"). Her husband, Henry, was a combat surgeon, and she was inspired to write the song after the Battle of Fredericksburg. While the words hail Michigan's many natural charms, the song is more a celebration of Michigan's war veterans.

> *"A song to thee, fair state of mine,*
> *Michigan, my Michigan;*
> *But greater song than this is thine,*
> *Michigan, my Michigan;*
> *The whisper of the forest tree,*
> *The thunder of the inland sea,*
> *Unite in one grand symphony*
> *Of Michigan, my Michigan."*

—Opening lines of "Michigan, My Michigan"

 Seeing as how "Michigan, My Michigan" has a poached melody and outdated lyrics, a grassroots movement is currently afoot to make "A Beautiful Peninsula," a folksy ballad written by a retired nursing worker from Flint named Betty Wilkins, the new state song. Songs the rest of the world are more likely to associate with the state include the country classic "Saginaw, Michigan," the blues standard "Michigan Water Blues," "Detroit Rock City" by KISS and "Especially in Michigan" by the Red Hot Chili Peppers, along with anything from homegrown indie troubadour Sufjan Stevens's concept album *Michigan*, which includes such state-minded songs as "Flint (For the Unemployed and Underpaid)," "Say Yes! to M!ch!gan!," "The Upper Peninsula" and "Oh God Where Are You Now? (In Pickerel Lake? Pigeon? Marquette? Mackinaw?)."

State Birthday

On January 26, 1837, Michigan became the 26th state to join the Union. An Aquarius, the state shares a birthday with *The Sound of Music*'s Maria von Trapp, octogenarian sex symbol Paul Newman, hockey hero Wayne Gretzky, guitar hero Eddie Van Halen, slam dunk specialist Vince Carter, comedienne Ellen DeGeneres and that other guy from Wham!

DID YOU KNOW?

Elsewhere in the world, January 26 is celebrated as Australia Day (to mark the 1788 landing of the First Fleet in Sydney); Republic Day (to celebrate India's official independence in 1950 after nearly 100 years of British rule); and Liberation Day (the Ugandan celebration that marks the ousting of the murderous dictator Idi Amin).

State Flag

Michigan's first governor, 25-year-old, Virginia-born Stevens T. Mason, was known as "the Boy Governor" and was so proud of his big new job that he put his own portrait on the original state flag. The 1837 version featured Mason's mug on one side and Michigan's coat of arms on the other. The current flag, adopted in 1911, features only the coat of arms sitting on a dark blue field. The emblem's design sees a moose and an elk flanking a large shield, with the unlikely image of a waving man with a gun standing in front of a setting sun. The flag's three featured Latin phrases include the official U.S. motto, *E Pluribus Unum* ("Out of many, one"), the Michigan motto (see page 18) and, much larger, the word *Tuebor* ("I will defend").

State Quarter

Michigan's entry into the U.S. Mint's 50 state quarters series was carefully planned by a state-sponsored commission. There was concern that the Michigan quarter design would focus only on Detroit-area interests, like the automobile, and exclude the rest of the state. Other elements were considered, including lighthouses, the Mackinac Bridge and white pine trees. Some designs crowded as many as five distinct objects onto the quarter.

The final design avoided any specific imagery. Minted in 2004, Michigan's very own 25-cent piece features a map of the state with outlines of the four Great Lakes it borders and even the fifth one, Lake Ontario, which it doesn't.

Sister State

America's "Great Lakes State" shares a symbolic bond with Japan's "Lake Country", Shiga Prefecture. Located about 300 miles west of Tokyo on the country's main island, Shiga is home to Lake Biwa, Japan's largest lake and one of the ten oldest lakes in the world. A donated American paddlewheel steamboat named the *Michigan,* staffed by students from Flint Community College, now provides regular transportation across the lake's waters.

Turning Japanese

Fourteen cities and towns in Shiga are linked as "sister cities" with communities in Michigan, and the 15 public universities and colleges in Michigan regularly send students to the Japan Center for Michigan Universities (JCMU), located in the city of Hikone, to study the Japanese language and Japanese culture. Japanese students also study English at JCMU.

AVERAGES AND EXTREMES

They say there are only two seasons in Michigan: mosquito-swatting season and snow-shovelling season. Here are a few of the recorded extremes for both:

- Hottest Day: 112°F at Detroit on July 9, 1936

- Coldest Day: −51°F at Vanderbilt on February 9, 1934

- Rainiest month: 12.81 inches, September 1881

- Driest month: 0.06 inches, May 1986

- Warmest winter: Average temperature 30.9°F, 1877–78

- Coldest winter: Average temperature 5.1°F, 1978–79

- Snowiest day: 29 inches fell at Ishpeming on October 23, 1929

- Snowiest month: 133.7 inches fell at Delaware in December of 2000

- Snowiest winter: 390.4 inches fell at Delaware in1978–79

- Least snowy winter: 14.8 inches, Escanaba 1899–1900

- Biggest snowstorm: 61.7 inches fell at Sault Ste. Marie between December 8–11, 1995

Climate Range

Michigan's climate is considered semi-maritime because of the Great Lakes. They create a unique climate system known as "the lake effect," cooling the westerly flow of warm air during summer and warming cool air during winter. On average, a 10-degree temperature moderation occurs along the shores year-round, while more extreme temperatures occur inland.

- Average July temperature: 69°F

- Average January temperature: 20°F

- Average yearly precipitation: 32 inches

STORMY WEATHER

Twister Bout

Michigan's worst natural disaster was the Flint Tornado of June 8th, 1953. Rated an F5 on the Fujita 1–5 Scale of tornado intensity, the twister was the last tornado in the U.S. (to date) to kill over 100 people and the ninth deadliest tornado in the country's history. In the Flint region, 116 people lost their lives and 844 more were injured. Winds were estimated to be over 200 miles per hour, and the giant twister carved a path of destruction 27 miles long. Approximately 340 homes were completely destroyed, and the damage was estimated at around $19 million (about $125 million by today's standards). Although by far the biggest, the Flint Tornado was just one of eight tornados that hit the eastern portion of the Lower Peninsula that summer. The other seven caused an additional nine deaths and 52 injures. The resulting damage stretched from Alpena to Erie.

DID YOU  KNOW?

Yet another F5 struck again just three years later in and around Hudsonville, killing 17 people and injuring 130. Since 1953, 331 tornadoes have struck southeast Lower Michigan, killing 166 people.

The Great Storm of the Great Lakes

Few storms in American history can rival the one known as "The Great Storm of 1913" in terms of ferocity and loss of life. It first hit the Great Lakes region on November 7 at Port Huron. The infamous blizzard, with winds of up to 90 miles per hour, soon covered most of Michigan and neighboring Wisconsin. It took four long days before finally dissipating and claimed 19 ships and 248 sailors, 200 of whom were never seen again. Damages were estimated at around $5 million.

The Internet Diary of a Michigan Newcomer

August 12—Moved to Michigan. It is so beautiful here. The hills are so serene and beautiful. Can hardly wait to see snow cover them. God's country… I love it here.

October 14—Michigan is the most beautiful place. The leaves are turning all different colors. I love the shades of red and orange. I went for a ride through the beautiful countryside and spotted some deer. They are so graceful; certainly they are the most peaceful animals on earth. This must be paradise. Michigan, I love it here.

November 11—Deer season will start soon. I can't imagine any-one wanting to kill such an elegant creature. The very symbol of peace and tranquility. Hope it will snow soon…I love it here.

December 2—It snowed last night. Woke up to find everything blanketed in white; it looks like a postcard. We went outside and cleaned the snow off of the steps and shoveled the driveway. We had a snowball fight (I won), and when the snowplow came by, we had to shovel the driveway out again. What a beautiful place. Mother nature in perfect harmony...

December 12—More snow last night. I love it. The snowplow did his trick again (that rascal). Winter wonderland... I love it here.

December 19—More snow last night. Couldn't get out of the driveway to get to work this time. I'm exhausted from shovelling. Stupid snowplow...

December 22—More of the damn white stuff fell last night. I've got blisters on my hands from all this shovelling. I think the %@#$ snowplow driver hides around the corner and waits till I'm done shovelling my driveway.

December 25—"White Christmas." More friggin snow. If I ever get my hands on the SOB who drives that snowplow, I swear I'll castrate him. Don't know why they don't use more salt on the roads to melt the ice.

December 28—More %#$! snow fell last night. Been inside since Christmas Day, except for shoveling out the driveway after every time "Snowplow Harry" comes by. The weatherman said to expect another 10 inches tonight. Do you know how many shovels of snow 10 inches is?

January 1—Happy Frickin' New Year. The weatherman was wrong. Again. We didn't get 10 inches last night; we got 34! At this rate it won't melt before the 4th of July. The snowplow got stuck up the road and the SOB actually had the guts to come to the door and asked to borrow my shovel. After I told him I've broken six shovels already, shovelling all the snow he pushed into my driveway, I broke the last one over his head.

January 14—Finally got out of the house today. Went to the store to get food. On the way back, a stupid deer ran in front of me. I hit the $@#! and tore my car all up. Did $3000 in damages. They should all just be killed. Wish the hunters had killed all of them last November.

March 3—Took the car to the garage in town. Would you believe the thing rotted out from all the frickin' salt they keep dumping all over the road. Car looks like hell.

April 8—Moving back home again, I can't imagine why anyone in their right mind would ever want to live in a god-forsaken hole like Michigan.

An old Yooper joke describes weather in the U.P. as 10 months of good sledding and two months of poor sledding.

GENERAL GEOGRAPHY

The Pleasant Peninsulas

Michigan is the only state made up of two separate peninsulas. The Lower Peninsula, to which the name Michigan was originally given and where most people live, is known as "The Mitten," a nickname many believe fits like a glove thanks to the state's distinctive shape, with its obvious "fingers" and "thumb" areas. When asked what part of the peninsula they come from, residents often point to the corresponding part of their hand.

The Upper Peninsula is sometimes referred to as "The Slipper," which it barely resembles at all but is in keeping with the article of clothing motif. Residents certainly don't point to anywhere on their feet when asked what part they're from. The sparsely inhabited region is more commonly called the U.P., otherwise known as either "Da Yupé" or "Yooperland," and its residents are known as "Yoopers." The two regions are connected by the 5-mile-long Mackinac Bridge, which is the third longest suspension bridge in the world.

High Point

Michigan's mightiest mountain is part of the Upper Peninsula's Huron Range and is ranked 38th of America's 50 state high points. Mount Arvon, elevation 1979 feet, is located a few miles east of the town of L'Anse in Baraga County. Like nearby Arvon Township, Mt. Arvon takes its name from the deposits of slate in the area, which reminded early British immigrants, mostly miners, of those around Carnarvon in Wales. Although the mountain sits on private land owned by the MeadWestvaco paper company, hikers are welcome to climb it, but trees block views from the summit.

DID YOU KNOW?

Mount Arvon is located a few miles from Mount Curwood, which for years had been designated as Michigan's highest spot, until a resurvey in 1982 determined that Mt. Arvon is actually a foot taller than Mt. Curwood.

WATERWORLD

Michigan has the longest freshwater shoreline of all the states and more recreational boats than anywhere else in America. Michigan's territorial waters include 40,000 square miles of the Great Lakes, which combined hold 20 percent of the planet's fresh surface water. The two peninsulas are home to over 11,000 inland lakes, 37,000 miles of rivers or streams, and more than 150 waterfalls.

Four Out of Five Ain't Bad—Michigan's Great Lakes

☛ **Lake Superior** - the lake was named "Lac Supérieur," meaning Upper Lake, by early French explorers because it was located above Lake Huron, but the name has proven serendipitous. Lake Superior, at 31, 800 square miles, is the largest freshwater lake in the world by surface area. Lake Superior is found along the shores of the Upper Peninsula.

☛ **Lake Huron** - the waters of Lake Superior empty via the St. Mary's River into the second largest of the Great Lakes, Lake Huron, which sits along the eastern shores of The Mitten's index finger and thumb. The 23,010-square-mile lake is named for the Huron tribe who first lived in the region.

☛ **Lake Michigan** - Lake Huron and Lake Michigan are separated by the narrow Straits of Mackinac and technically are the same body of water. Lake Michigan is the only Great Lake without a Canadian shoreline. The lake is famous for having the world's highest freshwater sand dunes and beaches with "singing" sand made of fine silica that makes a distinct scrunching sound when stepped on.

☛ **Lake Erie** - Michigan only accesses a small stretch of the southernmost Great Lake, and its share of Lake Erie's shores is mostly shallow and marshy. The Erie name comes from the Erielhonan tribe who once lived along the lake's southern shore. The tribe has the distinction of having been wiped out by fellow Native Americans rather than by white settlers.

A Good, if Not Great, Lake

Michigan actually has a fifth shoreline lake, though it is not actually one of the Great Lakes. Lake St. Clair sits between Lower Michigan and Ontario, to the north of the Detroit River and to the south of the St. Clair River. The lake is small by Great Lake standards (only about 430 square miles) and shallow (its maximum depth is only 21 feet, with an average depth of 10 feet). It is so shallow, in fact, that the state had to dig shipping trenches so that heavy freighters could travel across without scraping the bottom.

 All Michigan schoolchildren know HOMES, the mnemonic device for memorizing the Great Lakes. The letters stand for Huron, Ontario, Michigan, Erie and Superior, which is great for remembering their names, but terrible for memorizing their locations on a map. Lake Ontario is represented, even though it does not border Michigan, and Lake St. Clair, which does, is conspicuously absent.

Uncommon Roscommon

Michigan's largest inland lake is found in Roscommon County in the upper Lower Peninsula or, more specifically, near the second knuckle of The Mitten's middle finger. Houghton Lake covers over 20,000 acres and is one of the largest completely natural inland lakes in America. It is an extremely popular year-round fishing destination and the site of Tip-Up-Town USA, a large annual ice fishing and winter sports festival. The name originates from the flag-like devices, "tip ups," used for ice fishing. Held two consecutive weekends in January, the festival's big draw is the $25,000 price on the head of the legendary Wally the Walleye, a giant fish that has been frustrating fishermen for years.

Rio Grand

The longest river in Michigan is the Grand River. The state's longest waterway runs 260 miles east through the cities of Jackson, Lansing, Grand Rapids and Grand Haven before finally reaching Lake Michigan. Originally named Owashtanong by the Ottawa tribe, meaning "faraway water" because of its length, the river drains an area of 5570 square miles and was once an important navigational route through the Lower Peninsula used by various Native American tribes and later by early European explorers and settlers.

Grand Theft

The Grand also formed a major boundary in an historic real estate deal. In the 1821 Treaty of Chicago, the Ottawa and Potawatomi nations gave up their rights to all lands in Michigan Territory south of the river, with the exception of several small reservations.

DID YOU  KNOW?

The city of Grand Rapids no longer has any grand rapids. Although the riverside city sits 610 feet above sea level and is only 30 miles from Lake Michigan, a series of dams and locks have eliminated the whitewater that gave the city its name.

Tea-Colored Falls in a Forest

Michigan's highest waterfall is also the second highest falls east of the Rockies, after the rather better known Niagara Falls. Located near Lake Superior in the eastern Upper Peninsula, Tahquamenon Falls drops nearly 50 feet along the Tahquamenon River and is more than 200 feet wide. During the spring freshet, the river drains as much as 50,000 gallons of water per second. The falls are located in a state park that is named after them, and a paved half-mile pathway leads from the parking lot through an old-growth forest to an observation platform at the crest of the falls. Because the headwaters of the river are located in a boreal wetland that is rich in cedar, spruce and hemlock trees, the river carries large amounts of tannin and is often brown or golden brown in color. The Tahquamenon Falls are accordingly acclaimed as the largest naturally dyed or colored waterfall in the country.

The Tahquamenon River was mentioned in Henry Wadsworth Longfellow's epic and much parodied 1855 poem "The Song of Hiawatha." " In the solitary forest, by the rushing Taquamenaw" is where the titular Ojibwa chief built his famous canoe.

If You Seek a Pleasant Isle

The largest island in the world's largest freshwater lake is Michigan's only national park. Isle Royale National Park was established in 1940 and was made an International Biosphere Reserve in 1981. A roadless, wilderness archipelago made up of a 210-square-mile main island and about 400 surrounding islands, it is known for its wolf and moose populations. There are usually around 25 wolves and 1000 moose on the main island, and this makes for an ideal outdoor lab for scientists to investigate predator-prey relationships in a closed environment.

Royale Treading

Visitors to Isle Royale National Park have to really want to get there. Fewer than 20,000 people visit per year—fewer than the most popular national parks see in a single day. Access is limited to the summer months via float plane or ferry from Houghton and Copper Harbor in Michigan or Grand Portage in Minnesota. The park isn't a popular destination for day-trippers; ferries are a 6–7 hour round trip and are often canceled because of bad weather. The remote isle features 165 miles of hiking trails, including Isle Royale's crown jewel, the 40-mile Greenstone Ridge Trail running from one end of the island to the other.

DID YOU KNOW?

One of the more popular activities on Isle Royale is swimming out to Ryan Island on Siskiwit Lake, which is the largest island in the largest lake on the largest island in the largest freshwater lake in the world.

The Dunes

The Sleeping Bear Dunes National Seashore stretches across 35 miles of Lake Michigan shoreline, from Crystal Lake in the south to Good Harbor Bay in the north (on The Mitten's "little finger"). The park, created in 1970, is a natural beauty, with a mixture of sandy beaches, forests and even two islands. Its namesake feature is its giant sand dunes, which dominate the lakeshore atop already imposing glacial moraines (ground features cut by retreating ancient glaciers). There are three main dune areas: Empire Bluffs, Sleeping Bear Bluffs and Pyramid Point. Many people are surprised to learn that the dune sand actually comes from below rather than sliding from above:

waves crashing against the moraines expose sand and gravel, and winds from off the lake lift the sand onto the dunes.

There is plenty of hiking, sightseeing, swimming, kayaking and dune climbing (probably the single most popular activity at Sleeping Bear). Even in a cold Michigan winter, park trails are open to snowshoe hikers and cross-country skiers, and there are even opportunities for hunting and fishing.

Since no visit to Sleeping Bear Dunes is complete without a telling of its famous legend, here it is:

The Legend of Sleeping Bear

One day, a great fire erupted along the western shore of Lake Michigan, driving all of the animals out of the forest. A mother bear and her two cubs dove into Lake Michigan to escape the flames. They swam towards the eastern shore, but the cubs were slow, and they quickly got tired. The mother bear made it to the eastern shore and stayed there on the lookout for her two cubs, but they never came. The bear cubs drowned, and their bodies became the islands of North and South Manitou. The mother bear stayed at her post, refusing to give up on her cubs. She became the dunes at Sleeping Bear Point.

 Michigan author Kathy-Jo Wargin and illustrator Gijsbert Van Frankenhuyzen created an illustrated children's book, *The Legend of Sleeping Bear*, in 1998. The book has quickly become a favorite of local children and was named the Official State of Michigan Children's Book.

SOME INTERESTING MICHIGAN CRITTERS

Bald Eagles

Yes, Michigan is year-round habitat for the nation's treasured (but once endangered) symbol, the bald eagle. The birds are more common in the Upper Peninsula but also nest in the northern Lower Peninsula. They avoid urban and suburban areas, and so almost never nest in the most populated parts of the state.

DID YOU KNOW?

The bald eagle was chosen as our national bird because of its beauty, independence and fierce reputation. But at least one Founding Father, Benjamin Franklin, disliked the choice, noting that the bald eagle is also a scavenger, more likely to live off the efforts of others rather than hunt for itself. Franklin wanted America to embrace the wild turkey instead, which he said was more honest, moral and dignified!

Eastern Massasauga Rattlesnake

Michigan is home to only one poisonous snake, and even it is pretty rare. The Eastern Massasauga rattler spends its winters in wet, swampy hovels, waiting for the temperature to rise. In the summer months, it roams drier, less populated areas of the Lower Peninsula in search of small rodents and other prey. It dislikes confrontation and will generally bite humans only if they startle it or if it cannot escape otherwise. Because of its timid nature, most Michiganders go their entire lives without seeing one outside of captivity.

 The most famous feathered Michigander isn't a goose as might be expected, but rather a rooster. In Michigan, the answer to the age-old question about why chickens cross the road might be because that way their blood keeps circulating and their feet don't freeze. This was a lesson learned the hard way by a rooster in Jackson one winter in 1996 when his feet froze beyond fixing. Fortunately for him, he was befriended by a local vet, who named him "Mr. Chicken" and introduced him to a physical therapist who built a pair of acrylic feet to fit over his stumps. Mr. Chicken became an instant celebrity after his story was told in *Newsweek* and in newspapers around the world.

Sadly, the legless rooster's fame was cut short. In June of 1997, only six months after receiving his new appendages, he was found mauled to death, most likely by raccoons, while trying to protect the hens that shared his pen. But at least Mr. Chicken died with his boots on.

Lake Sturgeon

One of the most ancient living fish species, the lake sturgeon inhabits the waters of the Great Lakes. Instead of scales, bony plates protect these ancient fish. The sturgeon once lived in abundance in the Great Lakes and roamed as far as Niagara Falls. Unfortunately for the sturgeon, it's tasty when smoked and its oils useful, so it has been widely fished. Although it is not considered endangered, its natural population has shrunk considerably and is confined to the less fished waters. Sturgeon farms also raise the fish for market.

DID YOU KNOW?

Sturgeons can grow to enormous sizes; the lake sturgeon can reach more than 8 feet long and weigh over 800 pounds, and it is far from the largest sturgeon in the world. Because of their bony plates and funny, pointed noses, large sturgeons have been suggested as the culprits behind sightings of the Loch Ness Monster and other lake monsters.

Skinks

There's only one kind of lizard in Michigan, the skink, though it exists in two subspecies—the common five-lined skink and the rare six-lined skink. These small, darting lizards are named for the light beige-to-yellow stripes that run the lengths of their bodies. The five-lined skink is abundant throughout the state, but the six-lined skink is limited mainly to the Thumb area.

MICHIGAN'S MOST ENDANGERED SPECIES

Clubshell and Northern Riffleshell

These freshwater clams' days are mostly up in the waterways of Michigan. The clubshell (*Pleurobema clava*) and northern riffleshell (*Epioblasma torulosa rangiana*) both require swift-moving and well-oxygenated water to survive. They require clear waterways and actually aid in the cleaning by filtering out sediment, which in turn attracts fish that prefer not to get their gills clogged. The clubshell is currently known to exist in 12 streams, and the northern riffleshell is restricted to the Detroit and Black rivers. In 1992, a "Rescue the Riffleshell" program transplanted 110 mussels into the St. Clair River in the hope they might re-establish. They didn't.

Eastern Puma

Hunted almost to extinction east of the Rockies by the early 20th century, with the last confirmed kill in Michigan occurring at Newberry in 1906, eastern pumas (*Puma concolor couguar*) might be making a bit of a comeback. This subspecies of puma is officially only found in Texas and Florida, but there have been a number of unconfirmed sightings in Michigan as well as Missouri, Kansas and Ontario. The most compelling evidence for its returned existence out east is, sadly, positive DNA evidence taken from the front bumper of a Kentucky man's car. If they did come back to Michigan, their return would drastically cut down on the number of collisions with the out-of-control deer population, which no longer has natural predators.

Gray Wolf

Gray wolves (*Canis lupus*), also known as timber wolves, are the largest member of the Canid family, which also includes coyotes and foxes. Although they once roamed throughout all of Michigan, gray wolves were hunted to extirpation in the Lower Peninsula by 1910 and were almost completely wiped out in the Upper Peninsula by 1960, when a state-paid bounty on wolves was repealed. It was almost too late because no wolves were seen at all in the ensuing decades until the 1990s, when a pack of 20 or so appeared, most likely having come from Ontario or Wisconsin. Since then, the wolf population has grown to an estimated 400 to 500, thanks largely to a successful education campaign to convince trigger-happy Yoopers to stop killing them.

Hungerford's Crawling Water Beetle

Found only in Michigan and neighboring Ontario, Hungerford's crawling water beetle (*Brychius hungerfordi*) is thought to be a relic from glacial periods when cool, fast moving streams were more common. This tiny, yellowish brown beetle is now only found in a handful of unpolluted streams, often below beaver dams or similar structures that provide some cover from hungry birds.

Indiana Bat

Although you might expect the Indiana bat (*Myotis sodalis*) to still be found in Indiana, today its remaining habitat is solely southern Michigan. This medium-sized, dark brown/gray bat is difficult to distinguish from other bat species, especially the more common brown bat. Reasons for the Indiana bat's decline include shrinking forests and suburban sprawl; this bat roosts only under the bark of trees in old growth forests, whereas more practical bats prefer buildings or other structures.

Kirtland's Warbler

Kirtland's warbler (*Dendroica kirtlandii*), a small, multicolored songbird, has the misfortune of nesting only beneath juvenile jack pine trees, which mainly grow only in Michigan. Not only have vast swaths of jack pine been chopped down, but the trees only spring up after forest fires, which are now prevented from occurring naturally.

Mitchell's Satyr Butterfly

Mitchell's satyr (*Neonympha mitchellii mitchellii*) exists only in 17 isolated areas of Michigan as well as two in Indiana. The largest factor in the satyrs' decline is that it only lives in rare freshwater wetlands called "fens," most of which have been drained and/or filled in to make way for urban and agricultural development. Butterfly collectors haven't helped much either.

Piping Plover

The wide-ranging piping plover (*Charadrius melodus*), a small, sandy colored shorebird, is considered endangered within the Great Lakes region and threatened in the remainder of its range along the eastern seaboard. The name is taken for its distinctive bell-like song, which is often heard before the bird itself can be seen as its coloring blends in with beach habitats. The piping plover's numbers are plummeting because of the loss of beach habitat and the damming of rivers, that eliminates sandbars and allows the growth of vegetation on its nesting areas.

A GANDER AT MICHIGANDERS

What's in a Name?

Michigan has an estimated population of over 10 million and is the eighth most populous state in the Union. Residents of Michigan are generally referred to as "Michiganders" although the terms "Michiganian," "Michiganer" and "Michiganite" are also occasionally used. Michigander was probably settled on because it most resembles the pronunciation of Michigan itself.

Grouping Yoopers, Lopers and Troopers

Then there are the names that residents of the Upper Peninsula have devised for themselves and their fellow Michiganders. In addition to proudly calling themselves "Yoopers," they call those from the Lower Peninsula either "Lopers" or "Trolls" (because they live "under the Bridge"), while Lopers who move to the U.P. are called "Troopers" ("Troll Yoopers") and residents on either side of the Mackinac Bridge are "Toll Collectors."

DID YOU KNOW?

The first recorded use of the term Michigander came from Abraham Lincoln. In 1848, Lincoln was running for president against Lewis Cass, a former governor of the Michigan Territory. Cass was campaigning on a platform that would have let states that were conquered in the Mexican-American War decide whether to legalize slavery. Lincoln, a Republican, accused the Democrats of exaggerating their feats in battle and simply riding on the coattails of former President Andrew Jackson. In a speech before Congress, Lincoln ridiculed Cass, implying he was as silly as a goose by saying: "But in my hurry I was very near closing on the subject of military tails before I was done with it. There is one entire article of the sort I have not discussed yet; I mean the military tail you Democrats are now engaged in dovetailing onto the great Michigander." The term stuck.

Original Michiganders

When French explorers first laid eyes on what is now Michigan, they encountered residents, the Algonquins, who'd already been living there for centuries. The Algonquins were loosely made of three main tribes—the Potawatomi, Ottawa and Chippewa—called the Council of the Three Fires.

Another native tribe inhabited parts of the state prior to the Algonquins. They're referred to as the Hopewell, after the Ohio farmer who first discovered their archeological remains; we don't know what they called themselves. The Hopewells lived throughout the Midwest some 2500 years ago. They are best known today from their elaborate burial mounds, several of which have been found in Michigan. Some of the best-known mounds are in Norton, near Grand Rapids.

But even the Hopewells weren't the first Michiganders. An ancient Copper Culture lived in the Upper Peninsula over 6000 years ago. These prehistoric peoples mined the copper in the U.P., which they used to make tools and weapons. Copper Culture artifacts were traded throughout the region.

FLOCKS OF MICHIGANDERS

Vanilla Flavored

Michiganders today are mostly white and Christian. According to the most recent census, 81 percent of the population identify themselves as Caucasian. Americans of German ancestry are present throughout most of Michigan, and people of Nordic (especially Finnish), British (notably Cornish) and French descent are particularly common in the Upper Peninsula. Western Michigan is known for its Dutch heritage (the highest concentration of any state), especially in the Grand Rapids-Holland area.

 The religious affiliations of Michigan are roughly 82 percent Christian (58 percent Protestant and 24 percent Roman Catholic), 2 percent Muslim and 1 percent Jewish. The remaining 15 percent are lumped together under Other.

What's 'hood for the Michiganders —
Michigan's 10 Largest Cities

Over half of Michiganders live in the greater Detroit area. All
10 of the state's biggest cities are found in the Lower Peninsula
and, apart from Grand Rapids and Lansing, all are located in the
sprawling southeast corner within shouting distance of each other.

Detroit

The Paris of the West. Motown. Motor City. Murder City.
Hockeytown. D-Town. The D. The 313. Founded by fur trad-
ers in 1701, Michigan's biggest city is now the 11th most populous city in the country. The current population of just under
one million is only half of what it was a few decades ago, the
result of a mass white exodus to the suburbs following race riots
in the 1960s. Detroit is now 80 percent African American. It is
the only major city in America where you can look south and
see Canada. Detroit's official motto is *Speramus Meliora;
Resurget Cineribus*, Latin for "We Hope For Better Things; It
Shall Rise From the Ashes," rather apt given the city's tendency
to catch and/or be lit on fire.

Famous Detroiters include boxer Joe Louis, aviator Charles
Lindbergh, baseball player Ty Cobb, missing Teamster boss
Jimmy Hoffa, novelist Joyce Carol Oates, director Francis Ford
Coppola and singers Aretha Franklin and Diana Ross.

Grand Rapids

The second-largest city in Michigan, "Bland Rabbits" is famous
for manufacturing furniture rather than cars, having a laid-back
Dutch attitude and many world-class outdoor sculptures (includ-
ing the city's signature *La Grande Vitesse* made by Alexander
Calder), and being just 30 miles from Lake Michigan's scenic
Gold Coast. A few Grand Rapidians made good include former
President Gerald Ford and his wife Betty, head Red Hot Chili
Pepper Anthony Kiedis, X-Files actress Gillian Anderson, R&B
music's DeBarge family and boxing's famous Mayweather family.

Sterling Heights

There isn't much of an elevation gain in the Detroit suburb of Sterling Heights; the name was arbitrarily chosen when Sterling Township was incorporated as a city in 1968 but there was already an existing Sterling in Arenac County. It is best known for being the site of presidential candidate Michael Dukakis' disastrous 1988 photo-op when the Massachusetts Governor, hoping to toughen up his image as a suitable commander-in-chief, was photographed sporting an overly large helmet and posing in a tank at the city's General Dynamics plant. "Dukakis in the tank" has since become shorthand for a backfired public relations appearance.

Warren

Ever see the movie *8 Mile?* Its depicts Warren as a grim "industrial/suburban" wasteland on the outskirts of Detroit that Rabbit, the autobiographical film's lead character (played by rap star Eminem) is desperate to escape from. Eminem, then known as Marshall Mathers, also grew up in Metro Detroit's largest suburb, graduating from Warren Lincoln High School in 1989. Needless to say, he doesn't live there anymore.

Flint

Flint is the largest city in the United States with a one-syllable name. According to the FBI, it is also a good place to get shot and has one of the highest violent crime rates in the country. Flint is known worldwide as being the birthplace of polemic documentary filmmaker Michael Moore, who first rose to fame with his 1989 film *Roger and Me*.

Lansing

Lansing is an unlikely state capital. Although Detroit had been the capital of Michigan Territory since its beginning, it was seen as being too far away from the rest of the state and too close to the hostile British and their Native allies across the river in Canada. Dozens of towns throughout the Lower Peninsula campaigned to become the new capital—with city fathers from the town of Marshall going so far as to build several mansions thought to be befitting a state capital—but tiny Lansing, at the time having a population of under 100 people, was instead given the honor in 1847, largely because the decision wouldn't benefit any particular political party. Lansing is also the only state capital that isn't even a county seat. Despite its modest beginnings, Lansing has gone on to produce such notable Americans as human rights activist Malcolm X, musician Stevie Wonder, NBA all-star Magic Johnson and Google co-founder Larry Page.

Ann Arbor

Ann Arbor is very much a university town. Leafy and lefty, it is
home to the main campus of the University of Michigan, one of
the nation's best public research universities, and students and
staff make up around half of the city's population. The city is
famous for producing public radio and Caucasians with dread-
locks. Notable Ann Arborites include poet Robert Frost, play-
wright Arthur Miller and punk rocker Iggy Pop.

Livonia

Named after a region in northern Europe, Livonia has the distinction of being the whitest city in North America, which is
somewhat strange when you consider that it is only a few miles

from Detroit, the continent's second blackest city after Washington, DC. Over 95 percent of Livonians are white. Coincidentally, the city also has one of the lowest crime rates in the country. Well-known Livonians include NHL all-star Mike Modano of the Dallas Stars and porn star Dani Woodward.

Clinton Township

This Detroit suburb is named for a prominent politician from New York. No, not Bill or Hillary. Clinton is named for the Clinton River, which was renamed at the first meeting of the Michigan State Legislature in honor of DeWitt Clinton, the popular governor of New York from 1817 to 1823.

Dearborn

While Livonia is America's whitest city, nearby Dearborn is the country's most Muslim. Michigan's 10th largest city has the densest concentration of Arabs outside of the Middle East. Nearly one-third of the city's 98,000 residents are of Lebanese and Iraqi descent, who first came to the area to work in the automotive industry. Signs written in Arabic are a common sight in the northeastern part of the city. It is also home to North America's largest and busiest mosque. Well-known Dearbornians include automobile inventor Henry Ford, rocker Bob Seger, actor George Peppard, fashion designer Anna Sui and all-star NHL defenseman Brian Rafalski.

STRANGE MICHIGAN

Women in white, cursed intersections and phantom lights—are you in a bad episode of *The X-Files*? No, you're in Michigan, the state some paranormal enthusiasts have called the most haunted in the U.S. Whether believers or skeptics, Michiganders everywhere enjoy getting goosebumps while listening to the state's many weird tales.

Spooky Cemetery

According to believers, the most haunted place in Michigan is the William Ganong Cemetery, sometimes called the Butler cemetery, in Westland. Located in the middle of suburban sprawl, this old cemetery is no longer open to new burials. It's too crowded with old burials—and, so the stories say, with old ghosts. They wander the grounds at night, rattling chains, scattering flowers and even encountering one another as they walk. The ghosts may be coming at the summons of local witches. Locals claim that black magic symbols and paraphernalia have been found around the grounds.

One particularly dangerous spirit is said to walk outside the cemetery gates. Legends say that nearly 30 years ago, heavy rains uncovered the skeletal remains of Alice, a blond-haired woman in a white dress. Since that day, she has taken to walking a specific stretch of road. Drivers coming upon her inevitably swerve, thinking she is a living woman, and many get into accidents. Locals have dubbed the spot the "Bad Curve."

The Spooky Old Bridge

Canton residents know well the stories of the Denton Street Bridge. One story says that a Victorian-era woman and her baby were murdered beneath the bridge. Another tale claims that a young man drove off the bridge after swerving in a game of "chicken." Whether none, one, or both legends are true, the bridge is the site of some spooky experiences. "Ghost lights," floating orbs that sometimes rush at oncoming cars like headlights, are said to plague the bridge. Some people claim that they can hear the cries of a baby from beneath the bridge, and others say that their windows have fogged up and baby footprints have appeared on the glass. A few have even reported the "Blue Lady," perhaps the ghost of the murdered woman, walking across the bridge.

Deep Mysteries

With so many lakes, it would be surprising if Michigan didn't have a few tales of lake monsters. The Ojibwa tribes were the first; their stories told of Mishipeshu, the horned, swimming cat monster that stalked Lake Superior and smashed canoes. Mishipeshu was connected to the Great Lynx god of the Ojibwa. The lake monster itself may be a symbol of the god's wrath or simply a personification of the danger posed by rough lake tides.

Modern Michiganders tell tales of another Lake Superior monster, Pressie, so-called because it's frequently spotted near the Presque Isle River. Pressie is said to be serpentine and whiskered, with a length of 30 feet or more. It's never been reported to attack the way Mishipeshu has, and in fact sightings have all but died off in recent years. There is one alleged photograph

of Pressie floating around, but it's far from conclusive. Farther south, Pressie has a sibling, Bessie (sometimes called South Bay Bessie), which swims the length of Lake Erie. Bessie's existence is no better documented than her Lake Superior sister.

Haunted Campus

Mount Pleasant's Central Michigan University is home to a surprisingly high number of ghostly legends, perhaps perpetuated by the school's annual "Legends of the Dark" tour. Below are two of the spookiest:

Lady in White

Carolyn Corey was a model student while she attended CMU in 1950–51. She went to her classes regularly, got high marks and even joined the Young Republicans. She would have been a promising alumna. But then tragedy struck: on a beautiful spring morning in early May, Carolyn was found dead in her Barnard Hall dorm room. The exact cause of death was never determined.

Not long after her death, the residents of Barnard Hall began seeing her spirit. She drifted sadly through the halls, dressed in the white nightgown she was wearing on the day she died. She was a completely silent spirit, as the new occupant of Carolyn's old room discovered the next year. Waking suddenly from troubled sleep, the poor girl saw Carolyn floating above her bed. The dead girl's lips were parted as if to scream, but there was no voice to accompany the sight… no voice, at least, until the poor resident screamed herself.

For 45 years, residents of Barnard Hall saw or sensed Carolyn walking among them. Sightings and occurrences ceased only when the building was razed in 1996 to make way for a parking lot, but even that may not have given Carolyn her final rest. Many are convinced that Carolyn escaped the demolition and now walks freely across campus. Recently, an ethereal woman was reported near the library, fading into the early morning fog. Carolyn, it seems, will be CMU's most persistent spirit.

Spiteful Spirit

Natalie, a resident of the second floor of Barnes Hall in the 1970s, was a shy and friendless freshman who never got along with her roommates. This may have been why she hung herself in the corner of her dorm room one lonely winter night. But as lonely, shy and friendless as she was in life, Natalie has come to demand attention in death. Residents of her former Barnes Hall room must put something in the corner where she died or she becomes an unholy nuisance in their lives. Items go missing, especially homework; alarm clocks get switched off; posters fall off of walls; computers crash and electronics malfunction; all to get people to pay attention to Natalie.

In 1995, the residents of Natalie's room were watching the Miss USA pageant, and Natalie, not sufficiently entertained, decided to act out. Just as the program was about to crown the winner, she made the television go fuzzy. The television still worked—all the other channels were fine. But until the final credits had rolled on the Miss USA pageant, the girls could see nothing on that channel but ghostly static.

Ghost Lights

It's no surprise that many ghost stories are attached to Michigan's 116 lighthouses. We marvel at the beauty of light-houses in the daytime, but at night they can be downright spooky places—usually built in remote locales, all of which are waterside and therefore subject to high winds and crashing waves, with creaking machinery and lonely operators. In the wee hours of morning, strange sounds or unexpected glimpses could easily be the shadow or footstep of a lonely spirit.

Prior Resident

One such ghost resides at the Big Bay Point Lighthouse near Marquette, now a bed and breakfast. Although there's no way to know for sure, it is believed that five different ghosts haunt the B&B. The most active is the ghost of William Prior, a former lightkeeper who hanged himself after the death of his son. Prior startles guests by appearing and disappearing suddenly as well as by roaming the halls, closing doors and switching off lights. He usually appears as he did in life, a bearded man wearing a Lighthouse Service uniform.

Lonely Rock

Another Lake Superior lighthouse with ghost problems is Stannard Rock. This light is the remotest of the remote. It isn't even built on an island, but literally on a rock, one of a hazardous grouping in the shipping lane. The ghost is likely that of a Coast Guard engineer who was killed in an explosion shortly after the light was automated in 1961. Although no one staffs the station any longer, those sent out to Stannard Rock to maintain the light report an uneasy feeling, the occasional phantom sound or shadow and a strong desire to not remain after nightfall.

Keep the Light On

The Old Presque Isle Light near Alpena has what many would expect as the key feature of a haunted lighthouse: a ghostly light. This lighthouse has been out of service for years but became a popular maritime museum in the 20th century. One museum proprietor, George Parris, loved the old lighthouse, so much so that after he died in 1991, he may have returned to it. As a museum, the Old Presque Isle Light does not have a functioning light, but that has not stopped many people from reporting that they've seen one. The first was Parris's wife, Lorraine, but locals and travelers alike have since reported seeing the ghost light, including an Air National Guard patrol.

SUPERSIZE MI – A FEW OF MICHIGAN'S BIGGEST THINGS

World's Biggest Bronze Horse

Five hundred years ago, Leonardo da Vinci dreamed of creating a 24-foot-tall bronze horse statue for his patron, noted horse-enthusiast Duke Ludovico Sforza of Milan. Alas, this dream crumbled, along with the cast for his enormous equestrian effigy, after an invading French army used his full-size clay model for crossbow practice. Despite his many remarkable accomplishments, some biographical accounts claim da Vinci cried on his deathbed over not building the largest equestrian sculpture in the world.

The da Vinci Mode

In 1978, an airline pilot and sculptor named Charles Dent read about da Vinci's unfinished equestrian project in an issue of National Geographic and decided to follow in the master's footsteps. Dent raised $6 million to cast two 15-ton bronze stallions at a foundry in New York, working from da Vinci's sketches. One was given as a gift to the city of Milan in 1999, exactly 500 years after the French destroyed the original. The second casting, referred to as the "American Horse," now stands at the Frederik Meijer Botanical and Sculpture Gardens in Grand Rapids.

Super Scooper

Strategically placed behind the giant stallion is the world's largest poop scooper, a 12x12 foot aluminum shovel with a 22-foot wooden handle. It is debatable whether da Vinci would've approved of the addition, but at least his dream has come to fruition.

The Biggest Tire

Any traveler driving along I-94 between Detroit's city center and Detroit Metropolitan Airport has seen the Uniroyal Tire, the largest model tire ever built. This massive tire began as a Ferris wheel at the 1965 World's Fair in New York, where luminaries like the Shah of Iran and Jackie Kennedy took rides. After the fair it was moved to its present location along I-94 in Allen Park. The tire is 80 feet tall and weighs in at a massive 12 tons. So far, no one has built a car large enough for it!

The Western Hemisphere's Scariest Ski Jump

Suicide Hill, an artificial ski jump located on Pine Mountain's Copper Peak in the Upper Peninsula, is the largest jump in North America. Rising 176 feet above the top of the hill, the ramp allows for jumps of 600 feet, or about 35 percent farther than Olympic ski jumps allow. Hills larger than Olympic-size hills are known as "ski flying" hills, and Suicide Hill, built in 1970, is the only one of its kind outside of Europe. Ski flying is

currently a boys-only club, and the current world record, set
by Norwegian skier Bjørn Romøren in 2005, is a whopping
distance of 784 feet.

America's Largest Uncle Sam
Other states have Uncle Sam statues, but only Michigan has one
42 feet tall. The statue, which was built in California, has been
moved several times. It stood for many years in front of a Toledo
restaurant before a septic tank dealer bought it and painted its
hat and coat black to more resemble yet another Yankee icon,
Abe Lincoln. Uncle Sam is now located next to a gas station in
the town of Ottawa Lake, just north of the Ohio border. In 2001,
as part of the Hampton Inns' Save-a-Landmark program, he was
returned to his red, white and blue glory.

World's Biggest Stove

Measuring 25 feet tall, 30 feet long and 20 feet wide, the
world's largest stove made its debut at the 1893 World's
Columbian Exposition in Chicago. Oven making was once big
business in Detroit, before the auto industry eclipsed it, and the
oversized stove is a tribute to the Michigan Stove Company's
top-selling "Garland" model.

Factory superintendent William Keep
designed the huge stove and had it carved
in oak by an unnamed sculptor. Because it
is made of wood, nothing has actually ever
been burned inside the monster oven, which now sits perma-
nently on the grounds of the Michigan State Fair in Detroit.

World's Largest Collection of Dolls Dressed as Nuns
As a young girl, Sally Rogalski had the curious habit of dressing
her dolls in habits. Over the years, she and her husband Walter
amassed 230 dolls that they then dressed as nuns. In 1964, the
couple donated their collection to a Catholic shrine in the rural

Lower Peninsula community of Indian River on the condition the community never charge people admission fees. The collection has grown to 525 dolls and 20 mannequins, which represent various different diocesan clergy and over 200 religious orders of fathers, brothers and sisters. The doll collection even earned the official blessing of Pope John Paul II. The Catholic Shrine Doll Museum, located just off the I-75 highway, is hard to miss; it is located next to a 55-foot-tall crucifix, carved from a redwood tree and featuring a 7-ton bronze Jesus.

World's Biggest Bear Trap

Ed Sauvola built what he calls his "Tourist Trap" on the front lawn of his home in Chassell on the Upper Peninsula. The bear trap sculpture is 32 feet wide and 9.5 feet tall and features a snowmobile snapped in its jaws. Sauvola, a machinist for Michigan Tech University, was inspired to build the structure after a noisy snowmobile trail was built beside his property in 2004.

World's Largest Snowball / World's Largest Snowball Fight
One February 10, 2006, a grand total of 3745 Michigan Tech students, staff, faculty and friends in Houghton gathered together on the school's Sherman Field. There they set new world records by rolling a giant snowball 21 feet, 3 inches in diameter (eclipsing an earlier record of 16 feet, 9 inches) and taking part in the largest snowball fight in history (the previous record held by Wauconda, Illinois, was a mere 3084 combatants). They also set a new record for making snow angels, more than doubling a previous Bismarck, North Dakota, record of 1791, but that particular record soon fell when nearly 9000 vengeful Bismarckians gathered to plop themselves supine in the snow, wave their arms and legs and reclaim the title.

World's Hugest Hockey Crowd
After building a rink in the center of a football field, the biggest and loudest gathering of hockey fans ever gathered to watch the

so-called Cold War between archrivals Michigan State and the University of Michigan at Spartan Stadium. Mr. Hockey himself, the legendary Gordie Howe of the Detroit Red Wings, dropped the puck for the ceremonial opening face-off, and nearly 75,000 people watched the two teams play to a 3–3 tie.

World's Largest Limestone Quarry and Cement Plant

Limestone is a crucial raw material in making cement, so it is fortuitous that the two are found so close together on the Upper Peninsula. Rogers City has the quarry and Alpena the plant. You'll know when you're in Alpena because everything is covered with a light coating of what locals refer to as "pay dirt," hazardous dust laced with hydrogen chloride that is a by-product of making cement.

World's Largest Magic Shop

The small southern Michigan town of Colon bills itself as "the Magic Capital of the World." Colon's reputation as a magical Mecca began after an Australian named Percy Abbott visited the famous American magician Harry Blackstone, who had settled in the area. Abbott subsequently returned to town and started the Abbott Magic Novelty Company in 1933, which became the largest manufacturer of magical implements in the world. Every August, Colon also hosts a prestigious gathering, the world's largest annual convention of magicians, which magically doubles the town's population for a few days.

World's Longest Wooden Porch

Mackinac Island's Grand Hotel, designated a National Historic Landmark, first opened its doors in 1887 as a summer retreat for the wealthy. The massive 385-room Victorian hotel, already well known as the setting for the unveiling of Thomas Edison's first phonograph and the setting of the cult favorite film *Somewhere In Time*, is also known for being fringed with a 660-foot-long porch.

World's Chunkiest Chainsaw

Da Yoopers Tourist Trap, located on US-41 west of Ishpeming in the heart of the Upper Peninsula, is the home of Big Gus, listed in the Guinness Book of World Records as the world's largest working chainsaw. Twenty-three feet long and fired by a V-8 engine, the supersized saw sits on a rise overlooking the highway. The roadside attraction also features such additional reasons to pull over as a giant rifle mounted on a pickup truck, a 10-foot mosquito sculpture, a 60-foot model of an iron-mining drift, and a massive gift shop celebrating the Yooper way of life.

World's Largest Native American

A plaque at the foot of a giant statue of Hiawatha, located in downtown Ironwood in the Upper Peninsula, claims it to be the "World's Tallest and Largest Indian." This is technically incorrect. A skinny Abnaki in Skowhegan, Maine, has a good 10 feet on the 52-foot Hiawatha. Ironwood's bulkier Native American giant is, however, certainly the largest. Built out of fiberglass in 1964, Hiawatha weighs 16,000 pounds, including an internal steel frame, and was built to withstand 140 mph winds.

World's Hugest Hairball

The largest known hairball can be marveled at in Anthony Hall at Michigan State University's campus in East Lansing. The basketball-sized curiosity was fished from one of the four stomachs of a deceased Michigan cow many years ago.

World's Hugest Herd of Holsteins

Green Meadow Farms is one of the largest dairy operations in Michigan and has the largest herd of registered Holsteins on the planet. Located outside the town of Elsie, the 6500-acre farm is home to 9500 head of cattle, most of which are Holsteins, with a few Brown Swiss, Ayrshires, Jerseys and Dutch Belted cows thrown in for good measure. The family-run farm also doubles as the Michigan State University Training Center for Dairy Professionals and works with the school's Department of BioSystems and Agricultural Engineering to figure out how to turn cow dung into useable methane gas.

"MADE IN MICHIGAN" SOME OF THE STATE'S FOREMOST FIRSTS

First Class

America's first university was founded in Detroit in 1817, 20 years before Michigan became a state. Originally given the unwieldy name Catholepistemiad, the campus was built on 1920 acres of land ceded by the Chippewa, Ottawa and Potawatomi people. The territorial legislature paid $300 for the building, and professors earned $12.50 a year. The school mercifully changed its name in 1837 to the University of Michigan and relocated to Ann Arbor, where it became known as one of the top universities in the country.

First To Kill Death Penalty

In 1846, following the lynching of a Detroit man later proven innocent, Michigan became the first government in the English-speaking world to ban capital punishment. Most civilized nations later followed Michigan's lead, though in the United States only 12 other states have abolished the death penalty. Only Communist China and the Islamic Republic of Iran execute more of their citizens each year than America does, with a majority of executions taking place in Texas. A 2006 Gallup Poll shows death penalty support in the United States at 65 percent.

First Fair

The Michigan State Fair was the first of its kind in America when it began in 1849 at a field on the southwest corner of what is now Woodward and Duffield, just north of Grand Circus Park. Admission was one shilling (about 12 cents) and 14,000 people bought tickets to see the latest in prize-winning livestock and new-fangled farming machinery. In the early days the fair was held in a different city each year, but it eventually came to rest in its original location in 1905 after department store magnate Joseph L. Hudson and partners donated the 135-acre parcel of land. In subsequent years, the grounds grew to their present 165 acres—enough room to house the agricultural exhibits, a full-size rodeo coliseum, several amusement park rides, and a massive stage.

First to Break the Glass Ceiling
In 1889, Anna Bissell took over the Bissell company in Grand Rapids after the death of her husband, founder Melville Bissell. In doing so, she became America's first female CEO.

First Suburban Shopping Mall
The idea of a shopping mall was not new when J.L. Hudson Company opened Northland Center in Southfield in 1954. Northland was new, however, in its design—two enclosed floors of shops and boutiques, centered around a department store "anchor" (a Hudsons, of course), assuring customers one-stop shopping. It was the birth of the suburban shopping mall, a design that hundreds of malls in the nation have since copied. With its success has come criticism, however; many people blame the suburban mall for spreading suburban sprawl and drawing business away from traditional downtown shops. The mall itself has since been usurped by all-in-one box stores like Wal-Mart.

First Fireworks Ban

In 1929, Michigan became the first state to regulate the retail sale of fireworks. By law, Michigan retailers cannot sell any fire-work that explodes or launches into the sky, thereby dooming backyard Fourth of July parties to a sad lineup of fountains, sparklers,and snap pops. Each year sees an influx of Michiganders across the border into Ohio to buy the "good stuff," like rockets and Roman candles.

First Motor Voters

Michigan's 1975 "Motor Voter" law was the first in the nation to pair voter registration with driver's license renewal as a means to encourage voting. The idea was so good, it eventually got picked up at the federal level with the National Voter Registration Act of 1993.

First Land-Grant University

Michigan State University was founded in 1857 as the nation's first land-grant university and served as the model for dozens more later established under the Morrill Act of 1862. Originally named the Michigan Agricultural College, the school was the world's first institute of higher learning to teach scientific farming methods. Students were expected to put in three hours of hard labor each day to help offset costs. It is now the largest institution of higher learning in the state and one of the biggest in the country.

First High Stakes Pool

Detroit hosted the country's first national billiards championship in 1859. Mike Phelan of New York City defeated local hero John Seereiter to win a $15,000 prize, at the time an unheard of sum of money. The event was highly publicized in newspapers across the country, and stories about the bad blood between the two pool sharks turned the event into a media circus. Hundreds packed the billiard room at Fireman's Hall while thousands more stood outside.

First Soda

Vernors ginger ale, invented in 1866 by Detroit pharmacist James Vernor, is America's oldest soft drink. The story goes that Vernor was called off to fight in the Civil War in 1862, leaving behind a mixture of ginger, vanilla and spices he'd been working on sitting in an oak cask. When he got back, he discovered the drink had been changed by the aging process in the wood and declared the unexpected find "deliciously different," which remains the soda's motto to this day. A pungent golden ginger ale with a taste more similar to ginger beer than most ginger ales, Vernors is now manufactured and distributed throughout America by the Cadbury Schweppes corporation.

Locals often enjoy a Boston Cooler, which is Vernors poured over vanilla ice cream. The drink is named after Detroit's Boston Boulevard, not Boston, MS.

First Ski Jumps

The first ski jumping tournaments in the country were held in Ishpeming, a tiny mining community near Lake Superior, and were organized by Scandinavian immigrants who'd brought their homegrown sport with them. The Norden Ski Club, later renamed the Ishpeming Ski Club, hosted the first formal tournament on February 25, 1888. Jumps were built by pushing snow up against boards to form the scaffold, More snow was then piled up for the takeoff and smoothed out for the landing below.

First Submarine Railway

The world's first underwater railway tunnel was also the first of its kind between two countries. Built by the Grand Truck Railway in 1891 at a cost of $2.7 million, the 6000-foot St. Clair Tunnel under the St. Clair River linked Port Huron with Sarnia, Ontario. The project was a wonder of 19th century technology. Massive hydraulic jacks at both ends of the tunnel pushed forward circular shields. Workers who then shoveled out the earth were followed by others who lined the tunnel with circular cast iron sections. Only freight trains used the tunnel initially, and the first passenger trains began using it in 1892. The tunnel originally used only steam locomotives, but after a crew asphyxiated after being delayed inside, the tracks were electrified. The tunnel was sealed in 1994 after a wider adjacent tunnel was built.

First Coffee Substitute

A caffeine-free substitute for coffee sold by the Post Cereals that doesn't taste remotely like coffee, Postum was originally created by company founder C. W. Post in 1895. Post was a Seventh-day Adventist who believed caffeine was evil and so came up with a powdered alternative mostly made of wheat and molasses. It is arguable that the success of Postum arose largely from the ridiculous claims made by Post and his salesmen, who posed as medical experts and blamed coffee for everything from divorces to business failures and juvenile delinquency, as well as a dire condition called "coffee heart." Postum was also touted as a cure for appendicitis and other maladies, unsubstantiated claims the company refused to back down from until finally forced to by the Federal Trade Commission in 1951. It remains a popular choice amongst Mormons.

First Floating Post Office

Michigan is the only place in the world with a floating post office. Crewmembers of ships passing through the Detroit River can have mail delivered to them care of The J.W. Westcott II, Detroit, Michigan, 48222. Captain J.W. Westcott, who first ferried supplies to passing ships via rowboat, established the service in 1874. By 1895 he was delivering mail. All deliveries are now carried out by the 45-foot *J.W. Westcott II*, a vessel that provides Great Lakes freighters with 6000 pieces of mail a year. Deliveries are completed when freighters lower a bucket down to the smaller mail boat.

Neither Sleet nor Snow nor Sinking

On October 23, 2001, the *J.W. Westcott II,* sank underneath the Ambassador Bridge after being caught in the wake of a much larger ship she was serving. The captain and one other crewmember were killed while two more survived. The ship was later salvaged, refurbished and put back into service.

First Retail Giant

After discovering he wasn't cut out to be a farmer or teacher, Sebastian S. Kresge became a salesman and, in 1899, opened the first five-and-ten-cent store on Detroit's Woodward Avenue. Kresge went on to turn his half share in this store into 1346 more. By 1924, Kresge was worth approximately $375,000,000 (in 1924 dollars) and owned property worth around $100,000,000. In 1962, he opened the world's first K Mart.

First Paved Mile

The first mile of concrete pavement in America opened in 1909 on Detroit's Woodward Avenue. Although starting at Mile Zero would arguably have been more apt, the paved stretch was instead built between Six Mile and Seven Mile Road.

First Centerline

Eight years after the debut of the first paved road, the first yellow dividers were painted in 1917 on the state highway from Marquette to Negaunee Road. Signs had to be posted so that out-of-state drivers would know what the lines were for.

First Plow

Snowy Michigan also birthed the invention that allowed cars to be driven year round. Edward Levy, public works superintendent of the Upper Peninsula town of Munising, created the first practical highway snowplow in 1922. It was mounted on runners and consisted of two retractable wooden wings, each 10 feet high and 20 feet long.

First Highway

America's first intercity superhighway was built on an 18-mile stretch of Woodward Avenue between Detroit and Pontiac in 1923. It featured eight lanes and a 40-foot median for public transit service.

First Traffic Laws

It took a few years but the Michigan Legislature eventually realized in 1919 that these new-fangled automobiles can be dangerous and some oversight might be required. Michigan's early penalty system for careless drivers led to today's point system. Later on, Michigan was the first state to spell out traffic law instructions for drivers. "What Every Driver Must Know: A Summary of the More Important Rules of the Road" was published by Secretary of State Leon Case in 1937 and a million copies were distributed.

First International Tunnel

The mile-long Detroit-Windsor Tunnel built in 1930 was the first car tunnel between two countries. It is now the second busiest crossing between the United States and Canada after the nearby Ambassador Bridge. Around 28,000 vehicles drive through the tunnel each day.

First Interstate

Michigan was the first to complete a border-to-border interstate highway, the I-94, which runs 205 miles from Detroit to New Buffalo. It was completed in 1971.

First Booze-free State

Michigan was the first state to ban alcohol, deciding in the legislature in 1918 to become "dry" two years before national prohibition came into effect. Ironically, when the failed experiment with enforced sobriety came to an end in 1933, Michigan was the first to begin selling alcohol again. Julius Stroh of the Stroh Brewing Company (who'd been forced to get by in the meantime making near-beer, birch beer and even ice cream) poured the first newly legal pint in the country on May 10, 1933, at an American Legion convention in Detroit.

First Radio Station

Detroit station WWJ claims to be "the first radio station in the world to broadcast regularly scheduled programs." An estimated 30 homes received the station's initial transmission, which had a 100-mile range, on August 20, 1920. The broadcast began at 8:15 at night from the second floor of The Detroit News Building with the words "This is 8MK calling," followed by the playing of "Annie Laurie" and "Roses of Picardy." Two years later, the call letters WWJ were assigned; the first W for the newly-created Federal Communication Commission's ironic abbreviation for the eastern United States, and the following W and J for the first names of Detroit News owners William and John Scripps. WWJ 950 is now the city's only 24-hour all-news radio station.

First Air Service

Stout Air Services, a division of the Ford Motor Company, began providing America's first scheduled air passenger service on August 1, 1926. Stout flew regularly between Grand Rapids and Detroit and eventually expanded to include service to Cleveland and Chicago. Seven years later, Stout also became the country's first of many domestic airlines to go belly up.

First Black Nobel Prize Winner

Ralph Bunche, a diplomat from Detroit, received the 1950 Nobel Peace Prize for helping to reach an early armistice agreement between the Israelis and Palestinians. He was the first African American to win a Nobel Peace Prize and the first of many to be officially rewarded for trying to bring peace to a region that will probably never experience it.

First Fluoridated Water

In the early 1940s, scientists discovered that people who lived where drinking water supplies had naturally occurring fluoride levels had fewer cavities. In 1945, Grand Rapids became the first city in the world to add fluoride to its water supply. A six-pillar, white marble monument along the river walk between Pearl and Fulton Streets, on the east bank of the Grand River at the end of Louis Campau Promenade, celebrates the momentous occasion.

First Pedestrian Shopping Mall

The Automotive State became the unlikely birthplace of America's first pedestrian shopping mall when the city of Kalamazoo decided to close downtown Burdick Street to traffic. Built at the modest cost $60,000, the Kalamazoo Mall was seen as marking a new era for American city planning when it was constructed in 1958 and imitators soon sprung up in many other cities. Unfortunately, though popular with skateboarders, it proved to be a failed experiment for other Kalamazooians and the street was reopened to cars in 1998.

First Black Dean

When Clifton Wharton was appointed president of Michigan State University in 1970, he became the first African American to run a major American college. Wharton's most lasting contribution to the school was the completion of a new center for the performing arts. Dedicated in 1982, the theatre is named in honor of Wharton and his wife Dolores. After serving as president for eight years, he then became the head of the largest university system in the nation, the State University of New York, and after that left academia to become Bill Clinton's Deputy Secretary of State, the first African American to ever hold this second-highest foreign policy post.

First Female Little Leaguer

Carolyn King became the first girl to play Little League baseball when she took the field as a member of the Ypsilanti Orioles on May 8, 1973. King, who was 12 at the time, had to not only beat out 15 boys for a starting position but also had to take on the league itself. After head office withdrew the Orioles' charter for allowing her to join the team, Ypsilanti city council sued them for sexual discrimination, which eventually led to the forced cancellation of the league's boys-only policy.

First Bottle Bill

Michigan became the first state to require a deposit on drink containers to reduce waste and litter. The 1976 "bottle bill" was the first in the nation to provide for a 10-cent deposit for recyclable drink containers. Michigan still has the highest refund in the country, with most other states only offering a 5-cent incentive to recycle a container.

First Dr. Death Patient

Dr. Jack Kevorkian, a Michigan pathologist and euthanasia pioneer, assisted with the suicide of his first patient, Janet Adkins, who was suffering from Alzheimer's disease, at a campground in Oakland County in 1990. He was subsequently charged with murder, but the judge refused to allow the charge to proceed to trial, on the grounds that Adkins was the one who ultimately killed herself. Kevorkian claims to have assisted the deaths of over 100 more patients before a Michigan jury found him guilty of second-degree homicide in 1999 and sentenced him to 10 to 25 years in prison. In December 2006, it was announced Dr. Death would be paroled the following June because of a terminal illness.

First Niagara Falls Swimmer

In October 2003, Kirk Jones of Canton Township became the first and only person to survive a plunge over the falls without any safety equipment. After climbing over a railing and jumping into the water 100 yards above Horseshoe Falls, he plunged 170 feet into the water below. Jones miraculously survived the ordeal with only two fractured ribs and some bruised vertebrae. After passing up a lift from the stunned crew of the "Maid of the Mist" tour boat, he managed to swim to the Canadian shore to be met by waiting policemen. He was later fined $2300 and forbidden from ever entering Canada again, either by land, air or waterfall.

DID YOU  KNOW?

More than 3.6 million gallons of water pours over Niagara Falls every minute, flowing at an average rate of 100,000 cubic feet per second; five times the average flow of the Colorado River through the Grand Canyon. Around 5000 people have died either by accident or suicide at the falls since records began being kept in 1854. Of those, five were attempting stunt descents, usually taking the plunge in barrels or inner-tubes, and, more recently, even in a kayak and a jetski inadequately rigged to a parachute. Kirk Jones is one only 10 people to survive the plunge.

First Priestess
Joan Heneveld was ordained in 1976 as the first female priest in the Episcopal Church. Fifteen years later, she became the first female canon (meaning a priest who serves a cathedral) at Detroit's Cathedral Church of Saint Paul.

First Female Hall of Famer

In 1987, Motown singer Aretha Franklin became the first woman to be inducted into the Rock and Roll Hall of Fame. "The Queen of Soul," whose voice has also been declared one of Michigan's official natural resources, has won 19 Grammy awards (including an unprecedented 11 for Best Female R&B Vocal Performance, eight of them in a row) and has had two number one hit songs: "Respect" in 1967 and "I Knew You Were Waiting (For Me)," a duet with George Michael, in 1987.

First Online Voting

To avoid the pitfalls of dangling or pregnant chads, Michigan became the first state to use the internet to vote in an election. Over 46,000 registered Democrats used the new system in a February 2004 election that saw Senator John Kerry win the presidential nomination caucus. Michigan residents were required to apply for a paper ballot that could be used to vote online through a username and password included on the ballot. In addition, voters had to provide personal information such as a mother's maiden name, birth date or driver's license number.

...AND FINALLY, A MICHIGAN LAST.

Last Trick

Famed magician Harry Houdini gave his last performance at the Garrick Theatre in Detroit. Prior to his Detroit performance, Houdini had been performing in Montreal, Canada. Houdini often bragged that he was excellent physical condition and could take any punch to the stomach. This was partially true; if Houdini knew the punch was coming, he could tighten his muscles and brace for the blow. A Montreal student decided to test Houdini's claim, but didn't bother to warn the magician—instead, he sucker-punched Houdini four times in the stomach. One of the punches ruptured Houdini's appendix, flooding his body with bacteria. The pain was immediate, and infection soon followed, but Houdini completed his scheduled performances and continued on to Detroit.

When Houdini mounted the stage at the Garrick on October 24, 1926, he was running a fever of 104°. Still, he gave what was, by all reports, a typically grand performance. After the show, Houdini was admitted to Grace Hospital. Doctors attempted to treat him, but the infection was too advanced. He died six days later, on Halloween. The official cause of death was peritonitis resulting from appendicitis.

LOCALLY GROWN AND MADE

Good Eats

From the breakfast table straight through to desert, Michigan is a state defined by what it eats. A true Michigan meal is a plate full of good meat, locally grown produce and plenty of flavor, all in good-sized portions with a favorite local beverage to wash it down. There are local delicacies galore, not to mention a worldly collection of international cuisines brought by waves of immigrants from across Europe and Asia.

With great food comes great responsibility, however, and Michiganders may be a little light on the latter. Michigan residents have a weight problem! In recent years, the state has ranked between the 6th and 11th heaviest states in the union. Detroit, especially, weighs in amongst the fattest cities.

Michigan Cherries

Who doesn't love a Michigan cherry? There are many varieties grown in Michigan, with names like Attika, Gold, Napoleon, Hudson and Emperor Francis, but most people simply group them into two kinds, "sweet" and "tart." Michigan is the top U.S. producer of tart cherries and fourth in the nation for production of sweet cherries. Overall, Michigan produces more cherries than any other U.S. state. Michigan sweet cherries are sold to be eaten raw but are also processed into products such as ice cream, yogurt and maraschino cherries. Michigan tart cherries are rarely eaten as is and instead are used in recipes or manufactured into commercial products like jams, jellies and pie fillings. Tart cherries are also gaining popularity for their perceived health benefits.

MAGNIFICENT
MICHIGAN
It should come as no surprise that Michiganders throw an annual party for their most famous fruit. The National Cherry Festival takes place in Traverse City, drawing half a million visitors and 25 million dollars to the area every year. Local businesses and resorts happily get into the week-long celebration, which takes over the entire city. Annual events include the obvious cherry-related contests, including cherry pie eating and the Cherry Pit Spit, but there are also parades, art fairs, foot races, car shows, lakeside volleyball tournaments and golf shoot-outs. There's even a Cherry Queen coronation at a black-tie gala ball. The date changes from year to year, but the ball usually occurs around the July 4th holiday, just before the start of the cherry harvest.

MADE IN
MICHIGAN
Twice in history, Michigan was home to the World's Largest Cherry Pie and the World's Largest Cherry Pie Tin. Charlevoix was the first to wear the crown. The towns-folk baked their pie in 1976, using 5000 pounds of cherries and a specially made pie tin with a diameter of over 14 feet. In 1987, nearby Traverse City successfully stole the Charlevoix title with a pie that measured over 17 feet in diameter (baked during the National Cherry Festival, of course). Both pies have since been beaten out (by Oliver, British Columbia, in 1990), but the pie tins and records of achievement are still proudly displayed by their respective homes.

Apples

Michigan is one of the leading apple producers in the world, trailing only Washington and (sometimes) New York. One thousand orchards produce more than 20 kinds of apples, including familiar varieties like Macintosh, Red Delicious and Northern Spy. Apples rank as the state's most valuable fruit crop, account for more than half of its fruit crop tonnage and can bring in upwards of $100–150 million annually. Sixty percent or more of these apples are processed into sauces, pies, juices and other products, adding even more value to the crop.

Drink Your Apples

Michiganders also love apple cider, the tart and tasty drink made by pressing fresh apples. Cider mills operate throughout the state, producing hundreds of thousands of gallons of fresh apple cider each year. Tourists and locals alike flock to these mills each autumn to buy apples and cider, enjoy the state's beautiful fall foliage and even pick out a pumpkin for Halloween—almost every cider mill in Michigan also has a pumpkin patch. Most cider mills also sell deep-fried donuts, cooked fresh onsite, as the preferred snack of cider drinkers.

Never anger an apple cider fan by calling it "apple juice." The so-called "cider" sold in many national supermarkets is practi-cally juice, but real cider is unpasteurized and unfiltered, giving it a cloudy look, a hearty body and a tart taste that sets it apart. The best ciders are locally produced and taste good cold from the jug or mulled with cinnamon and other spices.

Berries

Michigan is a berry friendly place. In addition to cherries, it is America's top producer of blueberries, providing nearly half of the country's annual crop. Strawberries grow in every county in Michigan, and "U-pick" self-serve is a popular way to harvest them. The state has also begun developing a burgeoning com-mercial cranberry crop, mostly in the Upper Peninsula.

Potatoes

Michigan isn't all about fruit, though. The state's number one moneymaking produce crop is the potato, especially the summer or "new" potato crop. Popular varieties include the round white, the russet and the golden, as well as some of the best potato chip varieties, such as the Snowden, Pike and Frito-Lay. The state is the number one producer of potato chip spuds, with 75 percent of the harvest ending up sliced, salted and bagged. Michigan has not one, but two festivals dedicated to the potato: one in Posen and another in Munger.

Beans

Even many Michiganders are surprised to learn that their state is also a major producer of beans. Specifically, dried beans, the kind you might soak for a pan of bean soup. Black beans, cranberry beans and adzuki red beans are some of the state's top varieties, though farms also produce kidney beans (light and dark), great northern beans, navy beans and others. Most bean production takes place in the Thumb area and in the middle of the Mitten.

BRAND NAMES FROM MICHIGAN

Better Made
No snack food aisle in Michigan would be complete without bags of Better Made potato chips. This local brand has stood toe-to-toe with the national brands since 1930 and enjoys strong regional popularity.

Faygo

Anyone born or raised in Michigan will be familiar with Faygo, the tasty pop that comes in plenty of unique flavors. The company was founded by Russian immigrants Ben and Perry Feigenson, who began marketing Faygo as the Feigenson Brothers Bottling Works in 1907. Their pop began as a local treat and even today, despite being owned by Florida-based National Beverages, Faygo has maintained its headquarters on Gratiot Avenue in Detroit. Many of Faygo's original flavors, including fruit punch, strawberry and grape, were based on recipes the Feigensons used for cake frosting. Today, Faygo is known in part for having lots of sweet and unusual flavors, such as pineapple, raspberry creme, key lime and a classic favorite, redpop.

 Faygo lays claim to coining the word pop as regional slang for soda. The word comes from the sound a classic soda bottle makes when opened. The word is predominant in the Great Lakes region, though it has seen use throughout the continental U.S.

Gerber

Parents everywhere owe a debt to Daniel Gerber, founder of the Fremont Canning Company and inventor of the first jarred, strained baby food. Actually, parents owe a debt to Sally, Gerber's seven-month-old daughter, because she was the one whose illness led a doctor to suggest cooked, hand-strained meals. Preparing the food at home was a chore for Gerber's wife but a cinch for the equipment at the company. Within a year, Gerber began marketing the strained baby foods, beginning with classic flavors like strained peas, carrots, prunes and spinach. The company hasn't stopped selling them since. Sally Gerber served as the company's first taste-tester (naturally) and eventually grew up to be a company vice president.

JIFFY

Most kitchens have at least one or two boxes of JIFFY baking mix on the shelf. Mabel White Holmes and the Chelsea Milling Company introduced the famous blue-and-white-boxed baking mixes in 1930 as a quick alternative to measuring and sifting. JIFFY Mix was the first on the market to combine ingredients into a baking mix and thus gave birth to the industry now dominated by such names as Bisquick and Betty Crocker. Although the JIFFY brand has gone national, every step of the manufacturing process, from the milling of grain to the boxing and shipping, is still handled at their Chelsea facilities, all under the watchful eye of Howdy S. Holmes, Mabel's grandson.

 The folks at Chelsea Milling Company have placed a 50-foot high image of their famous JIFFY box on the side of the Chelsea factory grain tower. The sigh is so large it can be seen from clear across town. Howdy S. Holmes himself had to petition the Chelsea Village Council for permission to mount the sign, which is larger than city zoning laws permit.

Kellogg's

This most familiar of cereal producers is stationed in Battle Creek, where cereal was, in fact, invented (as we've discussed elsewhere). The company is best known for such breakfast fare as Corn Flakes, Frosted Flakes, Rice Krispies and Eggo waffles, though it has expanded its product line in recent years to include "convenience foods" like cookies, cereal bars and fruit snacks. The Kellogg Company is the leading cereal producer, with annual sales of one billion and a worldwide market. In recent decades, Kellogg Company built an entire complex around their headquarters and production facilities, including factory tours and a family-friendly activities center called Cereal City, USA. Not many flocked to Cereal City, however, and the company closed it down in 2006.

MAGNIFICENT MICHIGAN On the second Saturday of June, Battle Creek hosts the World's Longest Breakfast Table. The Guinness-record-setting event began in 1956 and currently features a 2700-foot-long table at which more than 60,000 people can eat the most important meal of the day. Kellogg's sponsors the table, of course, and the company provides all of the cereal for the event.

Life Savers
For many years, these candy favorites were manufactured in the city of Holland. They were considered a real local treat, even though candy maker Charles Crane had invented them in Cleveland. Unfortunately, the sale of the company sent production to Canada in 2004.

Pizza Rivalry

By some strange coincidence, Michigan is also home to three of the top pizza chains in the nation. Domino's Pizza, the current number two of take-out and delivery pies, was founded by Ann Arbor entrepreneur and former Tigers owner Tom Monaghan. Current Tigers owner Mike Illitch founded Little Caesars, the number four pie house, in 1959. Finally, the number 11 pie provider, Hungry Howie's Pizza, was founded in Taylor in 1973 by James R. Hearn, who has never been, as yet, a Tigers owner (though you never know what might happen). Pizza Hut, the top pizza chain, is stationed in Texas.

The Coney Dog

Ask any Detroit-area resident, and they will say that you haven't visited Detroit until you've had a Coney dog. Despite its New York-inspired name, these meat treats are pure Motor City. First take a hot dog—all beef, if you want it to be authentic. Put it in a bun, and cover it in Coney sauce, a kind of chili with no beans (this recipe can vary greatly from restaurant to restaurant).

On top of the sauce go onions and, if you're going for full authentic, yellow mustard. It's a hot dog so sloppy that many people eat it with a fork.

The Coney Island hot dog's creation is almost legendary. Two Detroit-area restaurants, American Coney Island and Lafayette Coney Island—which happen to be right next door to each other—both claim to be its birthplace. They were both once owned by Greek immigrant Constantine "Gust" Karos, who began by trying to recreate the sauerkraut-and-mustard dogs he'd eaten at Coney Island, New York. Lacking sauerkraut, he used chopped onions instead. One day, someone suggested that he ladle a scoop of the chili he served overtop the hot dog. It was the best suggestion Karos ever got.

 Coney dogs are called "Michigans" or "Michigan dogs" elsewhere, as in New York and Canada. The bean-free chili for the Coney is sometimes called Michigan sauce.

The Michigan Café

For tourists interested in sampling Michigan's wide palate, the Henry Ford Museum in Dearborn houses the Michigan Café, which specializes in dishes reflecting the tastes of Michigan. A typical daily menu features such items as a U.P. copper miner's pasty, Hamtramck cabbage rolls, Coney dogs, a Greektown salad, Vernors pound cake and Faygo pop.

Ladies and Gentlemen…the Pasty

The hearty, heavy, heavenly pasty is a staple of Yooper cuisine that has come to be appreciated all across Michigan. Essentially a hand-held meat-and-potato pie, the pasty has gone from sturdy miner's lunch to popular restaurant specialty since Cornish and Finnish miners made their way into the UP two hundred years ago. Recipes vary greatly from cookbook to cookbook and kitchen to kitchen, with some traditional recipes calling for everything from lamb meat and turnips to raw suet and lard. Below is a typical modern pasty recipe, adapted to today's tastes and cupboards.

CRUST:

3 cups all-purpose flour

1 stick unsalted butter, cut into pieces, chilled

1/2 cup shortening, chilled

1 teaspoon salt

1 cup ice water

1 medium egg mixed with 1 tablespoon water

FILLING:

1 pound coarse ground steak (venison or beef)

3/4 pound coarse ground pork (or beef, if using venison)

4 to 6 red potatoes, diced

1 cup rutabaga, diced

1 1/2 cups chopped onion

1/4 cup fresh chopped parsley

1/4 stick unsalted butter

Salt and pepper to taste

Place flour and salt in a large, chilled bowl. Cut butter and shortening into the flour until you have a coarse mixture that clumps when balled. Slowly add water, kneading, until dough forms and is not sticky; you might not use the whole cup. Cover the bowl with plastic wrap and chill for at least 30 minutes. While the dough chills, combine the filling ingredients in a large bowl, mix thoroughly and chill until the dough is ready.

When you are ready to assemble, preheat the oven to 400°F. Divide the dough into six equal chunks and roll them into 8–9-inch circles. Put 1 to 1 1/2 cups of filling on each circle, spreading it flat and leaving a half-inch lip. Wet the edges, then fold the dough over the filling and seal the pasty. Cut a small vent in the top of each one and brush the dough with the egg and water mixture. Line a baking sheet with parchment paper and place the pasties onto it. Bake them for about an hour or until the filling is fully cooked and the dough is golden brown. Let stand before eating.

MAGNIFICENT MICHIGAN

The annual PastyFest takes place on or around July 4 in Calumet, once a prosperous mining town and now a tourist destination. Events include a pasty parade, complete with marching bands, floats and, yes, even people in pasty costumes; competitions, including a three-legged race, a tug-o-war and a pasty cooking competition where chefs compete for the blue ribbon, bragging rights and a copper pasty trophy.

MAKING MICHIGAN

Founding French

In the 1500s, Michigan was part of "New France," the region of North America claimed by the French government. The first European on record to enter the state was Étienne Brûlé, a rugged French colonial. Brûlé first explored the region around the Saint Marys River in 1622 but chose not to stay—he wasn't interested in settling but in finding the Northwest Passage. It would be 46 years before another French voyageur, Jacques Marquette, founded the first permanent settlement in the state, Sault Ste. Marie. Over the next century, the French founded many new settlements, most of them as military forts and trading posts. Among them were Detroit, Marquette, Mackinac City, Saint Ignace and St. Joseph.

The French controlled Michigan until the Seven Years War (also known as the French and Indian War). During that conflict, the British invaded the region. In the end, Michigan, along with all of New France, was given over to British control in 1763.

The Rocky Road to Statehood

Over the next half-century, control of what was then referred to as "the Michigan Territory" remained largely uncertain. The British kept Michigan after the Revolutionary War, and for a time it was part of Canada. Under the 1793 Jay Treaty, some of Michigan was given to the United States...but then the area was retaken by the British in the War of 1812 and returned to the U.S. in 1814. Firm borders along the Great Lakes between the United States and Canada were not established until 1818.

The opening of the Erie Canal brought a wave of new settlers into the area, many from New York. New settlements were founded, and a territorial government was established. In 1836, Michigan decided to apply for statehood. Before it could be recognized, however, they had one more battle to fight: the Toledo War.

Holy Toledo!

It's not quite a case of Turtle Wax, but it turns out that the Upper Peninsula was given to Michigan as a giant consolation prize. When Michigan applied for statehood, only the Lower Peninsula was considered "Michigan." The "Toledo Strip" was also included within the state's borders. Ohio, already a state, objected—they claimed Toledo was theirs. Tempers flared, militias were marshaled and battle lines were drawn; but shots were never fired. The "war" was ultimately settled, after bitter diplomacy, by giving Michigan the Upper Peninsula in exchange for the Toledo Strip. Michigan was granted official statehood on January 26th, 1837.

DID YOU KNOW?

No one wanted the Upper Peninsula in 1837. One politician described it as "destined by soil and climate to remain forever a wilderness," and the giving of it was widely considered a slap in the face to the state. Luckily for Michigan, the area turned out to be rich in deposits of copper and iron! Though some modern Lopers would argue that the U.P. is basically still a wilderness...

Metal Country

In the 20th century, Michigan was best known for its automobiles. But in the 1800s, Michigan built much of its name, and its wealth, on its mining industry. In 1845, the Keweenaw Peninsula, itself jutting from the top of the Upper Peninsula, began mining its copper resources. The ore was plentiful and relatively easy to mine, and for 30 years, the Keweenaw was the nation's top producer of copper. It even earned the nickname "Copper County." As the Keweenaw mined out, deposits elsewhere in the U.P. were tapped, and mining continued through the turn of the century.

In addition to copper, iron ore deposits were discovered in 1844 around near Neguanee, Ishpeming and elsewhere in the western U.P. Large-scale mines were in place by 1849. For much of the late 19th century, Michigan was the nation's leading producer of iron ore.

Unfortunately, Michigan's mining superiority could not last forever. By the end of World War I, many of Michigan's copper and iron mines had been depleted, and the industry waned throughout the 20th century. The last copper mine closed in 1995, and only two iron mines remain open today.

HAILS FROM MICHIGAN

These are a few of the many people of note who began life as Michiganders.

William Edward Boeing (1881–1956)

This businessman founded the aerospace company that bears his name, the Boeing Company. He was born in Detroit.

George Armstrong Custer (1839-76)

Custer will always be the West Point general best remembered for his most ignoble defeat—the Battle of the Little Bighorn, which also resulted in his death. Citizens of Monroe will always remember him as their most famous local. He was born in Ohio but grew up in Monroe; he also met and married his wife there. Today, a street in Monroe bears his name, and historical plaques commemorate his time in the area.

Charles A. Lindbergh (1902–74)

"Lucky Lindy" is most famous for his historic transcontinental flight and for the kidnapping of his son. Though raised in Minnesota, Lindbergh was born in Detroit because his mother, a Detroit native, was staying with relatives at the time. He continued to keep ties with the city throughout his life, including a stint building B-24 bombers for Henry Ford during World War II. Today, several Detroit-area landmarks bear his name, including an airport and an elementary school.

Thomas Dewey (1902–71)

Thomas Dewey, best known for the premature newspaper headline "Dewey Defeats Truman," was from Owosso and attended the University of Michigan. He built his political career in New York, not Michigan, where he served as governor for three terms.

FREEDOM FIGHTERS

Michigan has long been a place for African Americans to find solidarity and support, from the days of slavery through the fight for civil rights. Many prominent African Americans were born in Michigan, and many more have come here in their fight for freedom.

The Underground Railroad

Before the Civil War, Michigan was fiercely anti-slavery. As part of the fight, it served as a stop along the Underground Railroad, the route that brought slaves to freedom in Canada. There were two routes through Michigan. The "Central Michigan Line" brought fugitives through the western part of the state, including Battle Creek and Jackson. The "Southern Line" came up through Ann Arbor and Ypsilanti. Both used Detroit, Wayne and Port Huron as crossing points into Canada. Many slaves came back after emancipation, and others stayed in Michigan once they arrived.

Sojourner Truth (1797–1883)

Truth began her life as Isabella, a slave in upstate New York. By the time she came to live in Battle Creek in 1856, she was already a famous voice for suffrage and emancipation, touring throughout the country. Truth continued to fight for those rights during her years in the state, including one incident in which she attempted to vote illegally in the 1872 elections. She was barred from the poll but not arrested. She died in Battle Creek, where more than 1000 mourners attended her funeral.

The "Black Eden"

During the decades of segregation between the end of World War I and the rise of the civil rights movement, middle-class African Americans flocked to the town of Idlewild in Lake

County. It was the only resort town in the Midwest open to black vacationers and landowners—in fact, Idlewild's four Caucasian founders went out of their way to create a black-friendly haven from the realities of segregation, selling plots of land for $35 each, with only $6 down payment. As a result, Idlewild became a "black Eden" for many years. It also became the center for many early civil rights movements, including the NAACP.

DID YOU KNOW?

Idlewild's clubs served as stepping-stones for some of the 20th century's most influential African-American entertainers. Big names who took the stage in Idlewild include Cab Calloway, Louis Armstrong, B.B. King, Aretha Franklin and Bill Cosby.

Rosa Parks (1913–2005)

Civil rights icon and all-around classy lady, Parks moved to Detroit in 1957, two years after her legendary refusal to give up her seat on a bus in Montgomery, Alabama. Her years in Michigan were some of her most productive in the civil rights movement, including her work with Michigan congressperson John Conyers and the founding of the Rosa and Raymond Parks Institute for Self-Development. She stayed in Detroit upon her retirement and until her death.

MAGNIFICENT MICHIGAN The bus on which Parks made her legendary stand remained in service for many years afterwards. It was retired in the 1970s, sold to a Montgomery-area man and parked in a field, all but forgotten. It wasn't until 2000 that the bus, now badly deteriorated, was "rediscovered" and acquired by the Henry Ford Museum in Dearborn. The bus underwent extensive restoration, and it is on display today.

Malcolm X (1925–65)

The radical civil rights advocate came to Lansing with his family in 1928, when he was four years old. In Lansing, his house was burned and his father killed by white supremacists. Soon after, his mother was committed to a Kalamazoo mental hospital, and Malcolm was sent to into foster care, where he stayed until leaving Michigan for Boston in 1941.

Malcolm X kept ties with Michigan throughout his life. He moved back to the area for a short time and even married his wife in Lansing. During his years in Harlem, Malcolm earned the nickname "Detroit Red" because of his Michigan connections (the "Red" came from the bright color he dyed his hair).

NOTABLE HAPPENINGS

The King of Beaver Island

Many Michiganders have forgotten Jesse James Strang (1813–56), whose delusions of power led him to become Michigan's first and only king. Strang was a Mormon leader and self-proclaimed prophet who split off from the Mormon Church in 1845 over doctrinal disputes. In 1847, Strang and his followers arrived on the Beaver Islands, near Mackinac, where they founded their own Mormon church. They also claimed they were founding a new kingdom of God. This did not sit well with the Catholic-dominated locals, who looked at Strang and immediately thought "cult."

Trouble arose quickly. The locals tried to cut Strang off from people and supplies, even paying local boat captains to refuse passage to and from Strang's island. Strang retaliated by calling the local Michiganders morally bankrupt. He claimed to have another holy vision and threatened a holy war. Then, on July 8, 1850, Strang had himself crowned king of the Beaver Islands—despite an attempted invasion by gun-toting locals to stop the coronation.

King Strang began his push to take over Michigan. The Mormons of Beaver Island formed a voting block with Mormons around the state, and they managed to get a Mormon state representative and court judge elected. But when Strang issued a stern warning to the state government in 1851—effectively declaring war against Michigan—the government could take no more. It was time to depose Michigan's king. In 1852, the Navy gunboat *Michigan* invaded the Beaver Islands. U.S. Marshals took Strang and 100 of his followers into custody.

Strang stood trial in Detroit. He was charged with a number of federal violations, including tax evasion. He stood as his own legal council, and despite old adages about fools for clients, he actually won the case. Strang and his followers were acquitted by a jury who felt the government was unnecessarily restricting religious freedom. Strang returned to the Beaver Islands and ruled there for four more years (as an elected official this time). However, his antics became too much for even his own followers; they assassinated him in 1846.

Local legend claims that Strang left behind a hidden treasure somewhere on the Beaver Islands when he died. There's little historical evidence for the riches, but some eager treasure hunters still search for it. If you're ever in the area, the most reliable stories say that Fox Lake is the place to look.

"Fire" at Italian Hall

One of the more tragic moments in Michigan history happened at Italian Hall, the miner's union hall in Calumet, the center of Copper Country in the U.P. In 1913, the miners were striking for more money. They had gathered with their families in Italian Hall for a union meeting, after which they threw a Christmas Eve party. During the party, someone in the small, crowded hall shouted "Fire!" The ensuing panic sent everyone stampeding out the door, of which there was only one, at the top of a narrow stairway. Seventy-four people were killed in the panic, more than 50 of them children.

Afterwards, the mine bosses were blamed for the panic. Locals accused hired thugs of starting the panic to harass the striking workers. They even accused the thugs of holding the doors of Italian Hall closed so that no one could get out. No such actions were ever proven, but the Italian Hall tragedy has sometimes been called the biggest mass murder in Michigan History.

DID YOU KNOW?

Folk musician Woody Guthrie commemorated the Italian Hall event in his song "1913 Massacre."

Detroit Riot

The civil rights movement in Detroit faced one of its ugliest days on July 23, 1967, when police raided an illegal bar in a black neighborhood. As they rounded up the bar patrons—all of them African Americans—crowds outside the bar began to pelt the paddy wagons with bottles and bricks. Someone broke a nearby store window. People shouted.

It was the beginning of a riot that would last more than a week. Race issues were forgotten for a time, as both white and black hoodlums used the riot as an excuse to vandalize, loot and set the city ablaze. Local authorities and the National Guard were both marshaled. By the time the riot was contained, 43 people were dead and more than 7000 were arrested. Damages to the city exceeded $50 million dollars.

The Fitzgerald Founders

On November 10, 1975, the 729-foot long, 13,500-ton steamship *Edmund Fitzgerald* was traveling from Superior, Wisconsin, to Detroit with a shipment of iron ore. As it neared Sault Ste. Marie, however, the *Fitzgerald* and an accompanying ship, the *Arthur M. Anderson*, encountered a Nor'easter—a terrible storm that churned the waters and sent 16-foot waves crashing over the decks.

To this day, no one is sure exactly what happened, nor what caused the *Fitzgerald* to begin sinking. Radio contact indicated that the boat was listing, but a distress call was never made and no certain cause has ever been identified. But sink she did, 17 miles from the nearest safe harbor and 10 to 15 miles from the *Anderson*. All 29 men went down with the ship. It is considered the worst maritime disaster to have ever occurred on Lake Superior.

DID YOU  KNOW?

In 1976, Canadian singer Gordon Lightfoot wrote a popular ballad, "The Wreck of the *Edmund Fitzgerald*," to commemorate the sinking. Lightfoot maintains tight control over where and when the song is played, making sure to honor the memories of the dead.

Dangerous Waters

More than 550 ships are known to have sunk in Lake Superior. Many have gone down on the stretch of lakeshore known as Shipwreck Coast, an 80-mile expanse beginning at Grand Marais and ending at Whitefish Bay. The stretch of water isn't particularly dangerous, but it is particularly busy, and the high traffic has led to an inevitable increase in shipwrecks.

IT'S *THE* PLACE TO VISIT!

Mackinac Island

Detroit may be the largest city, and Lansing the most important, but when it comes to singular communities in Michigan, Mackinac Island is the most unique. This island, which can only be reached via boat, is home to a bustling resort town that preserves a Victorian-era setting. The island has been a popular vacation destination for nearly 150 years. Today, it serves as a place for dining, dancing, hiking, biking and sightseeing. An old military post, Fort Mackinac, also draws crowds. Built in 1780, the fort once protected the Straits of Mackinac and saw combat during the War of 1812. It now serves as a historical museum.

Getting Around
Michigan may be the automobile state, but on Mackinac Island, cars are simply not welcome. Residents and tourists alike travel the island on foot, on bicycle, on horseback or in horse-drawn carriages. The only motor vehicles on the island are service vehicles, such as ambulances and construction trucks. There is no public gas station. Tourists who wish to do more than walk can rent bicycles, ride horses or hop on one of the island's many touring carriages.

MAGNIFICENT MICHIGAN

One of the most popular consumables on the island is Mackinac Island Fudge. The first fudge shop might have been May's Famous Mackinac Fudge, founded in 1930, though that claim has been disputed. Today, there are numerous shops serving up blocks of fudge in some 20 flavors, the most popular being "plain" fudge, which is chocolate. Residents don't purchase the treat in anywhere near the quantities that tourists do, so Mackinac Island tourists are sometimes labeled "Fudgies" by the locals. The fudge brings in big dollars, of course, and so an annual Fudge Festival has been founded to celebrate it (and encourage even more fudge sales).

Ain't It Grand?

The island's centerpiece is the Grand Hotel. It was built in 1887 by a consortium consisting of the Michigan Central Railroad, the Grand Rapids and Indiana Railroad and the Detroit and Cleveland Steamship Navigation Company, the first major hotel to be built on the Island. It was declared a National Historic Landmark in 1989.

The Grand Hotel is most famous for its porch, a building-length promenade that overlooks the island. At 660 feet, it is the longest front porch in the world. The porch's popularity increased after the release of the film *Somewhere in Time,* filmed in part on Mackinac Island. The porch is repainted every spring to keep it clean. Walking the porch, and indeed the halls, of the Grand is so popular that the hotel charges admission for non-guests to do so.

Rooms in the Grand Hotel are literally unique—none of its 385 guest rooms are alike. The most impressive are the "named rooms," including the upper-floor suites. Six of the suites were actually designed by former first ladies Kennedy, Johnson, Ford, Carter, Reagan and Bush (Barbara, not Laura), who were each given the opportunity to design a suite of their own. Rooms at

the Grand have seen such guests as Thomas Edison, Mark Twain, Esther Williams and five U.S. Presidents—Harry Truman, John Kennedy, Gerald Ford, George H.W. Bush and Bill Clinton.

The Grand is Mackinac's most notable draw, but it is not a hotel for everybody. Rooms start at $220 per night for small, windowless "Category 1" rooms, while the most expensive rooms can run as high as $665 on a weekend. A 19 percent gratuity is also added to all bills.

OTHER NOTABLE COMMUNITIES

Christmas

This Yooper town sits on the shores of Lake Superior and was so named because an enterprising gift maker built his factory here with dreams of making it the "new North Pole." The factory burned down and the man went out of business, but the name stuck. Today, Christmas is home to a large Christmas shop, Santa's Workshop, outside of which stands the World's Tallest Santa Claus (a 75-foot plywood St. Nick) and the World's Largest Concrete Frosty the Snowman.

Colon

This small town is the self-described "Magic Capital of the World." Legendary magician Harry Blackstone moved to Colon in the 1920s, and other magicians soon followed. The town gained a magic shop, Abbot's, in the 1930s and quickly began hosting an annual magician's convention, soon to enter its 70th year. Today, Colon is a well-known destination for prestidigitators at all levels of skill. Blackstone and 20-some other magicians have even chosen Colon as their final resting place, in the town's Lakeside Cemetery.

 The American Museum of Magic is in nearby Marshall. Located at 107 East Michigan Avenue, the museum displays many of Blackstone's stage props, plus plenty of other magical minutia. It also houses an extensive library of books and other reference materials on stage magic and magicians.

Frankenmuth

After finding itself bypassed by I-75 in the 1950s, Frankemuth reinvented itself as a regional tourist attraction. Drawing on the heavy German heritage of its community, the city has declared itself "Michigan's Little Bavaria." Frankenmuth has stamped its Bavarian flavor on buildings, streets and shops. Visitors to Frankenmuth can tour the World Expo of Beer, eat traditional German cuisine or purchase Bavarian cuckoo clocks and other Deutschland curiosities.

Frankenmuth is also famous for its chicken dinners. The Bavarian Inn and Zehnder's, two local restaurants, serve all-you-can-eat chicken dinners: . Between them, more than a million pounds of white and dark meat are served each year. Although not necessarily German, the chicken is delicious.

 Frankenmuth visitors can also shop at Bronner's CHRISTmas Wonderland, the world's largest dedicated holiday store. This year-round holiday boutique offers trees, ornaments, nativities and Santa Clauses of every size and shape, including decorations crafted expressly for their store. You can find Bronner's at, appropriately enough, 25 Christmas Lane in Frankenmuth.

Greektown

Greektown is a district in Detroit, considered a Historic Michigan District by the state. It was once the center of culture for Greek immigrants who arrived in the early 20th century, though today the area is primarily commercial. The main street is lined with Greek restaurants and shops, where tourists and locals can go for some of the most authentic Greek cuisine in the entire state.

Hamtramck

This Detroit suburb became a focal point for waves of Polish immigrants into Michigan in the 1800s. Today, its heritage has made it a hotspot for *paczkis,* pronounced "poonch-key," the indulgent pastry that Michigan Catholics (and everybody else) eats on Fat Tuesday. Hungry locals from throughout Southeast Michigan come to Hamtramak every year for the sweet treats, buying them by the dozen and often staying for the annual Paczki Parade. Yes, we said "Paczki Parade." For Hamtramck, Fat Tuesday is Paczki Day, and they don't let it go by quietly. They celebrate it with gusto, including music, polish dinners and a paczki-eating contest (the 2007 winner ate 15 of them).

DID YOU KNOW?

Paczki means "little package," a fitting description for this jam-filled pastry that was created to use up all the eggs, sugar and preserves in the house before Lent. And it's not just a doughnut; a real paczki is made from sugared egg whites, not the whole egg. Amongst the traditional paczki fillings is prunes, but fruit fillings like strawberry and blueberry, as well as Boston cream and even chocolate, are far more popular.

Hell

This devilishly monikered community, located in Livingston County, has embraced its name in good humor. And why not? Hell draws a lot of visitors each year, all eager to return home and exclaim that they "went to Hell and back." Hell caters to these tourists, offering them the Dam Site Inn for lodgings; the Screamin' Creamatory ice cream shop for those hot-as-Hell days; and a yearly Helluva' Cruise car show and parade. There is also an official post office, where every piece of mail is singed with fire (seriously!) and stamped with the phrase "I've been through Hell!"

No one is sure why the town has its infernal name. There's no official record of the naming, only a number of stories that the locals tell. One suggests that German settlers originally described the area as so *schön hell,* German for "bright and beautiful"; another accuses town founder George Reeves of flippantly saying, when asked what to name the place, "You can call the town Hell for all I care." We'll leave it to you to decide which theory seems more likely.

MAGNIFICENT MICHIGAN

Another famous "Hell" in Michigan was "Hell's Half Mile," the name given to a rowdy row of lumber-era bars in Bay City. The bars are more sedate nowadays, though the name lives on in the Hell's Half Mile Film Festival.

Holland

Holland was originally a Dutch settlement, named for the home country in Europe, so it should come as no surprise that Holland, MI, is also famous for its tulips. The flowers, which were imported along with the original settlers in 1847, grow by the millions in town, from the appropriately named Tulip Lane to nearby Windmill Island. The town even holds an annual Tulip Time festival to encourage visitors to come see the flowers in bloom (and to help pollinate the town economy). The festival takes place every May, and everyone is encouraged to look and to smell...but not to pluck. Picking tulips during the Tulip Time festival carries a fine.

Paradise

If a state has a Hell, shouldn't it have a Paradise as well? Although it hasn't embraced its name the way Hell has, this small community in the U.P. has several local attractions, any one of which can draw visitors. Paradise serves as the entrance to Tahquamenon Falls State Park, a popular hunting, fishing and camping destination. There are three lighthouses in close proximity, including the Whitefish Point Light, home of the Great Lakes Shipwreck Museum. And each August, the town holds an annual blueberry festival.

 Michiganders love to tell tales of the Boy Scout troop who set out to measure the distance between Paradise and Hell, only to find that it was actually 666 miles between them! The story is amusing but completely untrue. Michigan simply isn't large enough north to south (there are only about 600 miles of road between the tip of the Keweenaw and the Ohio border). The actual distance between Paradise and Hell is around 354 miles. And no, converting to kilometers doesn't help; it's about 550 of those. Driving 666 miles south of Paradise along I-75 will actually put you on the outskirts of Lexington, Kentucky.

Windsor, Ontario

Detroit shares a special relationship with its Canadian neighbor Windsor. Geographically, because of the way the land juts beneath Michigan's thumb, it is the only place on the entire U.S./Canadian border where you have to go south to enter Canada. There are two routes for heading south into Windsor: either across the Ambassador Bridge or through the Detroit-Windsor Tunnel. Thousands of residents of both communities take the international commute each day, and thousands of tourists travel across borders on evenings and weekends to eat at restaurants, gamble in casinos or just visit with friends and family. Because the legal drinking age in Windsor is 19, it has become a favorite of local college freshmen, too.

In celebration of the amity between the cities, Detroit and Windsor co-sponsor the International Freedom Festival each year around July 1. This weeklong celebration features events in both cities, including concerts, shows and a tug-of-war contest across the Detroit River. The event culminates in a huge riverfront fireworks display.

DID YOU  **KNOW?**

The Detroit-Windsor Tunnel was the world's first international automobile tunnel. It was built in 1930, using state-of-the-art construction techniques. It measures 5160 feet long, including 2200 feet of actual under-the-river roadway, which required the removal of more than 787,000 tons of earth. Nearly 30,000 vehicles drove through it in 2006, paying $3.50 each. While passing through the tunnel, drivers can listen to Detroit's WJR 760—the only station broadcasting on tunnel transmitters.

THE NAME'S THE THING

Ann Arbor

John Allen and Walker Rumsey must have been the two best husbands in the world. What other husband can claim to have honored their wives by naming a city for them? Both Allen and Rumsey had wives named Ann, and so they combined the name with the beautiful green groves, or arbors, that grew in the area, to christen the newly founded village Annarbor. The name was eventually split.

Colon

The town was named when a founder flipped open a dictionary, chanced upon the word "colon," and decided that the nearby lake and river system was shaped like the bodily organ.

Detroit

Literally, the name is French for "strait." French settlers originally named the site Fort Pontchartrain du Détroit, "Fort Pontchartrain on the Strait," for its location along the river connecting lakes Erie and St. Clair. It was named for Louis Phélypeaux, Comte de Pontchartrain, the same politician for which Louisiana's Lake Pontchartrain was named. Eventually, the "Fort Pontchartrain du" was dropped.

Escanaba

This community is named for *esconawba*, a Chippewa word meaning "flat rock," a reference to the flat rock bed of the nearby river. Coincidentally, there is also a city named Flat Rock in Michigan, south of Detroit, that is also named for the flat rock riverbed that runs through it.

Fenton

This city's name was based on the outcome of a poker game.
Three town founders had bet the naming of the town on the
match, and William Fenton won. Had the cards played differ-
ently, the town may have been called LeRoy or Rockwell.

Flint

The nearby Flint River, which was called Pawanunking, "the
river of flint," by local tribes because its riverbed contained a lot
of flint, was the inspiration for this city's name.

Frankenmuth

This name comes from the compounding of Franconia, a region
in Bavaria, and *muth*, the German word for "courage."

Hamtramck

This city was named after Jean François Hamtramck (sometimes Americanized as John Francis Hamtramck), the American
colonel who took command of Detroit in 1796 after the British
vacated it under the Jay Treaty.

Ishpeming

Originally, Ishpeming had the awkward name Lake Superior
Location (really). It changed its name to Ishpeming, after the
Chippewa word for "heaven" or "high place."

Kalamazoo

Named from the Native word *kikalamazoo*, "reflecting river," this
community's name is sometimes informally shortened to "the
Zoo," especially near the Western Michigan University campus.

Lansing

Named, in a roundabout way, for Revolutionary War hero
and Constitutional convention representative John Lansing, Jr.,

the city was actually named after Lansing, New York, which in turn was named for Lansing, the man.

DID YOU KNOW?

Many Michigan towns and cities were founded by settlers from New York, and so more than a few were named after an Empire State counterpart. Places with New York-inspired names include Auburn Hills, Genesee, Geneva, Ithica, Lansing, Livonia, Moscow, New Albany, New Buffalo, Rochester, Rochester Hills, Romulus, Salem and Saranac.

Mackinac/Mackinaw

City and island both take their name from the Native American word *michilimackinac,* variously defined as meaning "great turtle" (describing the shape of the island) or "place of the Michilimaki" (the ancient tribe who may have once lived there). There's no clear reason why the island is spelled "Mackinac" while the city is "Mackinaw," though both names are pronounced the same (MAK-in-awe).

Menominee

This city is named for the tribe that once lived in the U.P., though they no longer live in the region. The Menominee sold the land to the U.S. government in 1854 and were relocated to a reservation in Wisconsin.

Monroe

This city was named in 1817 to honor the newly elected president, James Monroe, who visited the territory that year. This bit of sucking up didn't garner the city any known favors from the White House.

Novi

There are a couple of stories that purport to tell how Novi got its name. One suggests that it is derived from "No. VI," as it was the sixth gate out of Detroit along a former toll road, or the sixth stop out from Detroit on the railroad. More likely, though, the name is derived from a Latin word for new, *novi,* suggesting that the city was a place to make a new start.

Paw Paw

Many locals get a chuckle out of this town's name, but few can say where it came from. The town is actually named for the nearby Paw Paw River, so-called by American Natives because its banks contain many paw paw trees. What's a paw paw tree, you ask? It's a tree that bears a fruit called a paw paw, sometimes called a Michigan Banana. A paw paw is a round, banana-ish tasting fruit (though it looks more like a kiwi) significant for being high in protein.

Sault Ste. Marie

In French, Saults de Sainte-Marie means "the Rapids of Saint Marys," referring to the rushing waters of the Saint Marys River, which the city overlooks. The name is often shortened to "the Soo," a name also applied to the Soo Locks that partition off the river.

DID YOU  KNOW?

Sault Ste. Marie is the oldest city in Michigan and one of the oldest European settlements in all of North America. It used to span both banks of the Saint Marys River. Today, the other half of the Soo is Sault Ste. Marie, Ontario, Canada.

Shiawassee

No one is sure what the name of this county means. It was originally the Native name for the river that twists through the county and may mean "twisting river," though no certain translation exists.

Traverse City

Early French settlers named this city after Traverse Bay, which was called la Grande Traverse, "the Long Crossing."

MAGNIFICENT MICHIGAN As you're traveling around Michigan's communities, you may need to ask directions. When you do, you will likely get "the Hand," a Michigander's always-on-hand state map: the right hand, upheld, palm out, representing the Lower Peninsula. Some enterprising locals may try to provide the Upper Peninsula as well, by sticking out the thumb, index, and middle finger of their left hand and holding it gun-like above their right hand. This is creative, but will leave them without a hand to give directions with!

THE GREAT OUTDOORS

Gone Huntin'

Hunting, fishing and other outdoor activities are high on the list of many a Michigander. Among game species in Michigan are deer (of course), ducks, pheasants, quail, turkeys, elk, badger, beaver, rabbit, skunk, crows and even bears. With such a wide range of game species spread across both peninsulas, it's no surprise that there is always something in season. With all the hunting going on, Michigan has had to explicitly protect certain animals from being hunted. These include eagles, hawks, owls and other non-game birds, as well as lynx, moose, martens, bear cubs and cougars.

Two Weeks of Good Hunting
Although there's good hunting throughout the year, the best two weeks of hunting—well, 15 days of hunting—come during

the last half of November. That's firearm season for deer hunting, a time so important to many Michiganders that they spend the entire year planning for it. An estimated 750,000 hunters head north each year, though only half of them will likely walk away with a kill. Firearm season is so popular that many schools and workplaces experience a sharp drop in attendance during the first week of rifle season. Some communities have actually declared the first days of hunting season an official holiday, and every year someone tries to get the state legislature to do the same.

Gone Fishin'

Trout is the most popular fish you'll find in Michigan's waterways, one reason why the brook trout is the state fish. Other common species in state waters include bass (both smallmouth and largemouth), walleye, northern pike, steelhead and salmon. And even a hard Michigan winter doesn't stop the anglers. Ice fishing is a popular cold-weather pastime, especially in the Upper Peninsula.

A local comedy troupe, Da Yoopers recorded what has become the unofficial anthem of Michigan deer hunters during firearm season: "The Second Week of Deer Camp." The song tells the tale of a typical Yooper hunting party, who spend more time drinking beer and playing cards than they do hunting deer. "It's the second week of deer camp," they sing, "the greatest time of year!"

Water Sports

Of course, one doesn't need to be targeting wildlife to have a good time. With more than 3000 miles of lakeshore, boating and water sports are at the top of many vacationers' lists. Over one million boats are registered for Michigan's waters, more than in any other state, and an estimated 40 percent of the state's population are boaters. The Grand Traverse Bay is a popular destination for boaters, as is much of the shoreline of lakes Michigan and Huron. Even winter's freeze doesn't stop an enthusiastic boater; during the cold winter, ski-bottomed, sail-powered iceboats skate their way across the lakes.

 The iceboat was a Michigan invention, probably inspired by the huge amount of frozen water the state sees every winter. The modern standard of iceboat design came out of a competition held by the Detroit News in 1936. Shipbuilder Archie Arroll submitted the winning design, known as the DN 60. The single-seat boat with three runners and a 60-square-foot sail is still the preferred model for iceboaters today.

Way Up North

Outdoor sports happen all over the state, but most outdoorsmen head "up north" for their hunting, fishing, camping and boating. They travel to the less urbanized counties in the northern Lower Peninsula and the Upper Peninsula. These parts of the state have much more undeveloped forest and open waterways, and thus have much larger populations of game and fish.

Hunting plays a role in Michigan's economy too, especially up north. Some towns are fully dedicated to the hunting season, with the success or failure of local businesses hanging on the arrival of hunters each year. The influx of deer and other game hunters into the northern counties injects an estimated $2 billion into local coffers.

RAINBOW PRIDE

Friendly Ferndale

Like most states, Michigan has developed centers of gay and lesbian culture. In the Detroit area, the city of Ferndale plays the part. Sometimes called "Fabulous Ferndale" or "Fashionable Ferndale," the suburb hosts the annual Motor City Pride festival, which draws more than 40,000 participants each year. Ferndale also houses Affirmations, a center for Lesbian/Gay/Bisexual/Transexual (LGBT) activism and community relations.

Gay Capital

Lansing has become another focal point for the state LGBT community. Some of the best LGBT bars can be found in Lansing and East Lansing (or so we've been told). Lansing, like Ferndale, also hosts an annual pride march, rally and festival, the largest in the state, organized by Lansing-based Michigan Pride. It is also home to the Lansing Gay Men's Choir and the Great Lakes Pride Band.

DID YOU KNOW?

The weeklong Michigan Womyn's Music Festival in Wahalla is a noted annual gathering for lesbians and feminists, the largest of its kind in America. It was founded as a lesbian gathering in 1976 and has grown into a cross-section of women's—sorry, wimmin's—culture. It is an event where a woman—er, womon—can express her own social and political voice amongst a group of like-minded activists. Leave your boyfriends at home, though; the festival is a male-free event, declaring itself a "womyn-born womyn space" (they've even barred male-to-female transsexuals in years past).

DRINKS AND DRUGS

Liquor Laws

All of Michigan's 83 counties are "wet." By Michigan law, alcohol can be sold only between 7:00 AM and 2:00 AM from Monday to Saturday, and Sundays from noon until midnight. The exception to this rule is January 1, when alcohol may be sold until 4:00 AM—a testament to Michigan's great New Year's parties! On the other hand, Christmas is the only day when alcohol sales are prohibited. A store or bar risks losing its license if it tries to spread a little "Christmas cheer" on Christmas day.

To this day, a Prohibition-era law on the books forbids consumers from carrying alcohol into Michigan from out of state and forbids out-of-state manufacturers from shipping their goods to residents directly. As a result, most alcohol manufacturers have established in-state bottling companies.

For 150 years, Michigan's hometown beer was made at the Stroh Brewery, located in Detroit. Viewed as a blue-collar beer, Stroh's sponsored Tigers radio broadcasts and was sold at Tigers games. Its brewery on Gratiot Avenue in Detroit was a local fixture until its demolition in 1985. Sadly, the company hit hard times and sold itself to out-of-state interests in 1999. The Stroh's label is still in use, but to many Michiganders, it's just not the same beer it used to be.

Detroit's River of Booze

During Prohibition, Michigan became a "dry" state two years before the passing of 18th Amendment. That did not stop Michigan from becoming the major route for Prohibition-era bootleggers. Perhaps following in the footsteps of their fur-trading ancestors, Canadian alcohol manufacturers began sending potables across the Detroit River. Stretching 28 miles long and littered with islands, the river was the perfect place to smuggle alcohol into the U.S. Seventy-five percent of the liquor brought into the country during the Prohibition came across the Detroit River. It came in boats, across the winter ice and even through an underground pipeline.

Hash Bash

Each year, Ann Arbor's "Hash Bash" draws thousands of die-hard marijuana smokers, as well as thousands of curious experimenters. This political rally and act of civil disobedience occurs in support of marijuana legalization laws. During the "Hour of Power," hundreds of people gather and light up marijuana joints in the streets.

Local legend suggests that Hash Bash was created by an Ann Arbor law that made marijuana legal on this day each year, but that's not the case. Ann Arbor marijuana possession laws are simply lenient, treating possession as a charge of civil infraction instead of a misdemeanor or felony. The charge for a first offense is a small fine of under $50. Several smokers are actually arrested during Hash Bash each year.

DRIVING INTO HISTORY

Jobs and Wages

Most Michiganders are employed in manufacturing jobs, such as at auto plants or parts suppliers; sales and marketing jobs, which includes everything from advertising to retail sales; and office jobs like clerks, accountants, dispatchers and receptionists. The top income producers include the manufacturing industry, along with agriculture and the tourism industry. The job areas experiencing the largest growth include high-tech jobs (Google recently opened offices in Ann Arbor) and life science jobs.

The economy is not all rosy for Michigan, though. In truth, Michigan has fallen on hard times in recent years. The manufacturing industry is shrinking as more factories find it cheaper to produce goods overseas. Many residents have lost their jobs and have struggled to find new ones. This has led to a 7.1 unemployment rate in 2006—49th in the nation, ahead of only Mississippi. The average Michigan income shrank to $32,735 in 2005, more than $2000 below the national average.

Show Me the Money!
So, where is the money in Michigan? The majority of it rests in the pockets of the bottom third of the state. The top money-earning county in Michigan is Oakland County, one of the Detroit counties, while the number two and three counties are Washtenaw and Livingston counties, which border Oakland to the west. The other two Detroit counties, Macomb and Wayne, rank 5th and 13th in the state. The capital county, Ingham, ranks 14th.

The U.P., in contrast, contains many of Michigan's poorest areas, including the poorest county, Luce. The one standout is Dickinson County, which ranks 19th in the state. The Dickinson County economy is based almost solely on its tourist trade—it has made itself a prime destination for everything from skiing and snowmobiling to camping, hunting and off-roading.

Driving Economy

Manufacturing—particularly automobile manufacturing—has been a driving force in Michigan for over 100 years. The "Big Three" American automakers all make their homes here: DaimlerChrysler in Auburn Hills, Ford Motor Company in Dearborn and General Motors in Detroit. During the 20th century, these automakers helped fuel the state economy. Unfortunately, the automotive industry has hit hard times. The woes of the Big Three have been big news, and the result has been a big hit for the state. Michigan's high unemployment rate can be directly connected to plant closures and automaker job buyouts. Manufacturing still tops the state job list, but fewer and fewer residents are employed in that sector each year.

One part of the automotive industry remains strong in Michigan, though: research and development. The state is home to more than 200 high-tech R&D facilities employing thousands of scientists and engineers. State analysts hope that these high-tech Michiganders will lure other tech-sector jobs to Michigan.

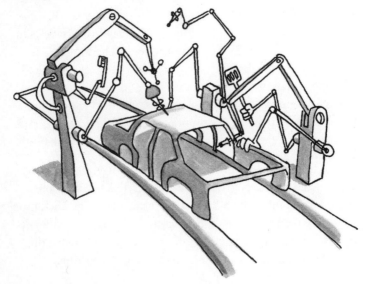

AND THE OTHER PAYING JOB?

Tourism Pays

Michigan has a burgeoning tourist economy. Its wealth of fresh-water shoreline has made it easy to establish lakeside resorts and beachfront campsites for swimming, boating, water-skiing, fishing and just about anything else that a visitor would want to do in the water. The Upper Peninsula has found particular value in such a tourist focus as a means of replacing the mostly died-out mining economy on which many towns were founded. Rivers and forestland in the U.P. are also powerful draws for outdoors tourists hoping to camp, hunt and fish.

Casino Power?

One bid to boost the economy in recent years came when then-governor John Engler passed Proposal E, opening the door for casinos in Michigan. The state was no stranger to casinos. There were 16 already operating in Michigan, many in the U.P., but they were all Native American–owned casinos on reservation lands, and little of the money flowed into state coffers. In addition, Windsor, Ontario, opened up a casino just across the river from Detroit, drawing many Michiganders to its game floor. So, the state thought, why not try to draw some of those high rollers to a casino that would benefit the state? Proposal E brought three casinos to Detroit: the Greektown Casino, the Motor City Casino and the MGM Grand Detroit Casino. Here's how they stack up:

Greektown

This casino is located on the edge of the noted ethnic neighborhood and has taken on the Greek theme in its decor. It has 2500 slot machines, 90 table games, three performance stages, four restaurants and 1600 guest rooms.

MGM Grand Detroit

There are no guest rooms at the MGM Grand's current location, which is a temporary casino, but there are 2800 slots, 78 table games, one performance stage and four restaurants. A permanent casino with 401 rooms is in the works.

Motor City Casino

The Motor City Casino has 2400 slot machines, 100 table games, two performance stages, three restaurants, and two lounges but, once again, no guest rooms. It also stands out as the only Detroit casino to have an entire game area—the third floor—declared smoke-free.

SOME STATE STATISTICS

Weight and See

Michiganders are overweight, probably as a result of all the good food we discussed a little earlier in this book. Recent surveys have ranked Michigan as the sixth fattest state, behind such states as Mississippi and Alabama (measurements vary from survey to survey, so it has also ranked as low as 11th). Detroit is especially heavy, ranking third in an annual survey, behind only Houston and Chicago. This has led to a series of state and local fitness initiatives in recent years in an attempt to create a slimmer Michigan. So far, they've met with limited success.

 Perhaps appropriately, Michigan was the home of the original Fat Lady—you know, the one who sings when it's all over. Her name was Lizzie Whitlock (1853–99), and she came from Batavia (though she may have been born elsewhere—the records aren't certain). By age 18, Whitlock weighed 500 pounds, a weight that eventually earned her a spot with Ringling Bros. and Barnum & Bailey Circus as part of the biggest, best-known freak show on Earth. Granted, Whitlock may not have been the first fat lady ever, but she was one of the best known; in addition to her weight, she was a skilled snake charmer. She topped the scales at somewhere around 650 pounds during her career. When she died (in Batavia) it took six men to remove her from her home.

Births and Deaths

Nearly 130,000 infants were born in Michigan in 2005. Their names were likely Jacob, Andrew, Emily or Emma—the most popular baby names in the state. Michigan's birth rate is close to the national average per capita.

The average Michigan male will live 72 years, barring accident or crime. The average Michigan female will live 78 years. These are, again, very much in line with the national averages. When the average Michigander dies, it will probably be of heart disease, the leading cause of death in Michigan. Heart disease accounts for nearly one-third of state deaths each year.

On an Average Day...

Here's a look at births and deaths on an average day in Michigan, as compiled by the state Department of Community Health.

- ☛ 347 babies are born, 28 of which have a low birth weight and 3 of which die.

- ☛ 225 Michiganders die; the most—68—die from heart disease, and another 55 die from cancer; only 9 die by accident.

- ☛ 3 people commit suicide

- ☛ 67 couples marry, either in churches or courthouses

- ☛ 95 existing marriages end in divorce

A SERIAL OF CEREAL

Welcome to "the San"

It was in the name of health that Battle Creek doctor John Harvey Kellogg and his brother, Will, invented a multimillion-dollar industry and forever changed the way we eat in the mornings.

Kellogg and his family were members of the Seventh Day Adventists, the sect of the Christian faith who believe in a Saturday Sabbath and a literal second coming. The Adventists established their first permanent church in Battle Creek in 1860. When the church rooted there, the Kelloggs followed. Little John was only four at the time. As he grew up in the church, Adventist leaders noted that he was an intelligent boy. They encouraged, and later helped fund, his medical education.

In 1866, the Adventists opened an alternative health spa in Battle Creek—the Western Health Reform Institute, later known as the Battle Creek Sanitarium. At the sanitarium, they encouraged Adventist health principles, including specialized diets, water therapies and frequent enemas. Kellogg joined the sanitarium in 1875 as their chief medical superintendent. His focus was on medicinal and surgical treatments, but he also became interested in diet and digestion, and "biological living" for better health. He promoted a regimen of diet, exercise and even correct posture as the means to healthy living, even writing several popular books on the subject. As his ideas spread, "the San," as it was known, became a popular retreat for the well-to-do.

Kellogg's most enduring idea came at breakfast time. He felt that meat and eggs, as many of his well-off patrons ate in the mornings, clogged the bowels. Kellogg wanted a grain-based, high-fiber breakfast for his patrons. His first creation was granola. But not the munching treat we know today, but a grain and cornmeal biscuit. He continued looking for new ideas, and in the course of his experiments, he accidentally discovered flaking, a means of cooking, drying, rolling and then re-cooking grain so that it cracks into flakes. Kellogg's brother, Will, who also worked for the sanitarium, soon applied flaking to cornmeal. The result was corn flakes.

Corn flakes turned into a sanitarium favorite, and in 1906, Will went on to market them to the public. To make them more palatable, Will added sugar to the batter, which Kellogg fought. The two argued violently over the subject; Will ultimately won the argument, but Kellogg never spoke to his brother again. Instead, he founded his own company, based on soy, but it was Will's Kellogg's cereals that endured. Today, the accidental discovery of flaking has led to a multimillion-dollar food industry.

A Postscript...

When C.W. Post visited the San, he was so inspired by the idea of cereal that he started his own company: Postum Cereal Co., now known simply as Post. His first cereal was Grape-Nuts (so-called because it contained grape sugar and had a "nutty" flavor), and he later marketed a competing product to Kellogg's Corn Flakes, called Elijah's Manna.

The Battle Creek/Lansing area is known as one of the nation's black squirrel habitats. The dark rodents are not natural to the area but were brought here by Will Kellogg, who preferred them to red squirrels and so set them loose on his family farm. The squirrels are best known for their common presence on the Michigan State University (MSU) campus, though they live as far north as the Central Michigan University (CMU) campus and as far east as Detroit.

BOOK SMARTS

Pioneering Librarians

Michigan has one of the finest library systems in the nation. Every county has an established library, as do most major cities. Many cities even have branch libraries of their own. Today, the Michigan eLibrary, or MeL, also keeps Michiganders informed. The credit for these great Michigan libraries can be given primarily to two women: Mary Spencer and Loleta Dawson Fyan.

Mary Spencer (1842–1923) is credited with creating a public Michigan library. Appointed state librarian in 1893, Spencer took the localized State Library of Michigan, accessible only to government officials, and made it a statewide library system open to all. She established associate libraries, to which state library books could be loaned, and traveling libraries, where small collections were loaned out to communities for up to six months. She brought books to the people.

Loleta Fyan (1894–1990) built on the system that Spencer established. She began her career in Wayne County, where she put into place one of the nation's first centralized county library systems. Then, in her 20-year tenure as state librarian from 1941–61, Fyan championed the establishment of such library systems in every Michigan community, including the rural areas that lacked any such resources. She handcrafted the modern Michigan library system, which is still in use throughout the state.

You might say that these two Michiganders wrote the book on libraries!

MICHIGAN SCHOOLS

The Largest Schools in Michigan

Michigan has 15 state universities, with an estimated total student population of 280,000. In addition, there are dozens more community colleges, private colleges and other institutions. Here are the top three schools in the state based on size.

The University of Michigan (U of M)

The undisputed king of learning in the state, University of Michigan (often simply "Michigan") boasts more programs, degrees and graduates than any other state school. Its 40,000-strong student body studies in over 200 programs at all levels from associates all the way up to doctorates. It is the oldest state-sponsored university in America, founded in 1817 (before Michigan even became a state!). It is considered the top school in Michigan and has been ranked as high as number two in the nation. Today it consists of three schools, each with its own campuses, admissions process and student body. The two smaller campuses are in Dearborn and Flint.

Of particular pride to the university is its football team, the maize and blue Wolverines. They were the first Rose Bowl winners, beating Stanford in 1902; since then, the Wolverines have earned 7 more Rose Bowl victories. They have also earned 11 National championships and 42 Conference championships.

DID YOU KNOW?

Michigan's football stadium is named simply Michigan Stadium, but it's better known as the Big House. It's the largest college stadium in the country, with a current capacity of 107,501. Even with all those seats, maize and blue fans still manage to make every game a sellout.

Michigan State University (MSU)

Second-place MSU always plays the underdog in Michigan, even though its student body of 45,000 is slightly larger than its rival U of M. The school was founded in 1885, and its primary campus is located in East Lansing. MSU can claim to be first in one respect: it was the nation's first land-grant university, a school founded on federal lands and charged with teaching agriculture, military tactics and engineering in addition to traditional academics. Today, MSU's Extension program, the outgrowth of these requirements, is one of the largest in the nation.

The school's colors are green and white, and its team nickname is the Spartans. Although Spartan athletics are some of the best in the state, they are generally considered second best to Michigan. The MSU's Spartans cannot boast the number of athletic trophies and titles that the rival Wolverines can. They do have a cooler mascot, though—Sparty the Spartan, a foam-headed, grimacing Greek warrior.

Baker College

The third-largest school is not a public university. It is private, not-for-profit Baker College, whose decentralized campus struc-ture has allowed it to prosper across the Lower Peninsula. Its home campus is in Flint, as is "the System," the umbrella under which Baker operates. Baker has grown steadily since its found-ing in 1888, both by establishing new campuses and by incor-porating local small colleges and business schools. It currently has 14 campuses across the state, such as Cadillac in the north, Muskegon in the West and three campuses—Allen Park, Auburn Hills and Clinton Township—in the Detroit area.

Baker College is very different from the public universities. It has no collegiate athletics, no team nicknames, no mascot and no social fraternities. It does have official school colors, bur-gundy and gray, though its website recently took a turn towards blue and green. Select campuses have dormitories, but the vast majority of Baker students are commuter students. Baker does not even follow the same semester system that the public univer-sities do, instead favoring four quarters of 10 weeks each.

OTHER PUBLIC UNIVERSITIES IN MICHIGAN

Central Michigan University (CMU)
Founded in 1892, this school is best known for its teacher's college and for its proximity to the Soaring Eagle tribal casino. CMU is located in Mt. Pleasant, the home of former governor John Engler. Its sports teams are known as the Chippewas, after the nearby tribe, though the school has ceased using its Native American chief mascot.

Eastern Michigan University (EMU)

EMU is located in Ypsilanti, very close to the University of Michigan. Its nickname is the Eagles, a moniker EMU adopted in the 1990s after it was pressured into dropping its former name, the Hurons (a local tribe). EMU was founded in 1849.

Ferris State University (FSU)
FSU is named for two-term Michigan governor Woodridge Ferris, who founded the school in 1884. A statue of the governor now stands in the middle of FSU's Big Rapids campus. The FSU nickname is the Bulldogs.

Grand Valley State University (GVSU)

GVSU is technically in Allendale, though anyone not from the immediate area just says that the school is in Grand Rapids, which Allendale abuts. The university was founded fairly recently, in 1960. GVSU's nickname is the Lakers, and their mascot is Louie the Laker, a Great Lakes sailor with a grimace like Popeye's.

Lake Superior State University (LSSU)

Founded in 1946, LSSU was originally a mining college. When all the U.P. mines dried up, the school, located in the Soo, had to upgrade its curriculum. Today it offers a variety of traditional fields of study, with some emphasis on environmental studies (wildlife management, environmental science, etc.). LSSU also uses the nickname the Lakers, and the school has two active mascots: Seamore the Seaduck (a blue-feathered waterfowl) and Fog Horn the Lake Superior sailor.

Michigan Technological University (Michigan Tech)

This school began, like LSSU, as a mining college before all the mines dried up. Michigan Tech has remained focused on science and technology fields of study, including engineering, computers and communications. It is located in Houghton. Michigan Tech is nicknamed the Huskies, and its mascot is Blizzard T. Huskey (the "T" stands for "The").

Northern Michigan University (NMU)

Marquette's NMU was founded in 1899 as a regional teacher's college. Today it is a broad-based university with more than 180 degree programs. NMU students root for the home team Wildcats with the help of their mascot Wildcat Willy, a big yellow bobcat.

Oakland University (OU)

OU is a suburban campus that has served Rochester and the surrounding areas since 1957. The school has a largely commuter population and is popular for its various cultural venues, including Meadowbrook Theatre, Meadowbrook Hall and Meadowbrook Music Festival. Its nickname is the Golden Grizzlies.

Saginaw Valley State University (SVSU)

SVSU is the new kid on the state university block; it was founded in 1963 as Saginaw Valley College and only became a state university in 1987. SVSU is technically located in the town of University Center, which is right next to Saginaw. Its nickname is the Cardinals.

Wayne State University (WSU)
Wayne State is Detroit's own university, located in the heart of the New Center district. As an urban school, WSU sees a lot of local talent pass through its doors. The school began in 1838 as a medical college, and its medical school is still strong today. The school's nickname is the Warriors, pictured as an armored knight with a sword.

Western Michigan University (WMU)
WMU was founded in 1903. Its current claim to fame is its aviation program, which is one of the largest in the country. The WMU Broncos are cheered on by mascot Bucky Bronco.

CAMPUS RIVALRY

U of M versus MSU

Each year, these top two Michigan schools face off in a great game that generates a lot of local loyalty. All U of M and MSU school alumni become stalwart loyalists on game day, while everyone else in the state chooses sides and dons the appropriate jersey. And well they should—a whole year's worth of bragging rights rest on this game, as does the Paul Bunyan-Governor of Michigan Trophy—a hideous 4-foot tall Paul Bunyan statue on a 5-foot-tall wooden base. As of 2006, U of M has dominated both series and bragging rights, with a series record of 66–28–5.

Michigan versus Ohio State

While the big MSU rivalry is a Michigan standard, this across-the-border gridiron contest is perhaps the most important football game of the year. Michigan pride is on the line, as Ohio has been a cross-border rival ever since the Toledo War. On the day of the big game, every Michigander is a U of M fan (except those who attended Ohio State). Ever since 1935, the Michigan vs. Ohio game has been the last game of the regular season, allowing it to take on even more importance, as the outcome of the game can decide the college football championship. In 2006, the two teams actually came to the game ranked number one and two, a first for the game; Ohio won in a stunning upset. In the long run, U of M fared better, with a winning 57–40–6 record.

 The most famous game against Ohio State was the November 25, 1950, "Snow Bowl" in Columbus, OH. A terrible snowstorm hit the stadium that day, and the entire game was played in blizzard conditions. The lines on the field were invisible, the other players were sometimes hard to see and the goalposts were blotted out from more than a few yards away. Michigan did not score a single first down the whole game, and all nine of their attempted passes were incomplete...yet they won the game 9–3, after a blocked punt tumbled into the end zone and a Michigan player fell on top of it first.

ODD SCHOOL

Red-Suited Recruits

Have you ever wanted to be Santa Claus? If so, you might want
to take a trip to Midland. That's the home of the Charles W.
Howard Santa Claus School, the oldest Santa school in the
world. The school was founded in 1937 in Albany, NY, by its
namesake, Howard (who served many years as the Macy's
parade Santa). The school's 40-hour, three-day curriculum provides prospective Santas with classes in proper Claus costuming,
Santa-like behavior and even the history of St. Nicholas.
Graduates receive a diploma and an invitation to return next
year for additional training. The Santa course runs $350 each
October—giving graduates plenty of time to practice before
Christmas.

STATE POLITICS

Blue Lakes, Blue People

Michigan is commonly known as a "blue" state, a Democratic
state with left-leaning politics. This has been true in the last
century or so, but it was not always the case. Prior to the Great
Depression and the rise of the automobile unions, Michigan was
a Republican state. Even today, the state is divided. Though it
has voted blue in the last 20 years and both of its Senators are
Democrats, only six of its 15 U.S. Representatives are Democrats.
This divide is fairly obvious from any election results map: the
highly populated and politically vocal urban and suburban lower
third of the state votes Democrat, while the less populated upper
two-thirds of the state (and one urban area, Grand Rapids) votes
Republican.

Governors

Michigan's governor's mansion has been occupied by 20 Democrats,
27 Republicans, two Whigs and one "Fusion" candidate (running on both the Democratic and the Greenback tickets). The
longest sitting governor was William G. Milliken (R), from
1969–83, followed by G. Mennen Williams (D) from 1949–61
and John Engler (R) from 1991–2003. Recently passed laws will
limit all future governors to eight years in office. Michigan's
oldest governor was Luren Dudley Dickinson (R), who took
office at age 79 and stayed in power only one year—and no, he
didn't die in office. The youngest was Stevens T. Mason (D),
Michigan's first state governor; the "Boy Governor" became
Michigan Territorial Governor at age 19 and was only 22 at the
time of statehood.

Michigan's governor as of June 2007, Jennifer Granholm (D), is the
state's first female governor and prior to that was the state's first
female attorney general. Granholm, though now a U.S. citizen, was
born in Canada. She was not Michigan's first Canadian governor,

though; Michigan has had one other Canadian-born governor, as well as a governor born in England and one born in Mexico.

Congressional Representation

Michigan is served by 17 members of the U.S. Congress, including two senators and 15 representatives. A single House member represents the entire population of the Upper Peninsula and Northern Lower Peninsula because of the very low population density in the north. Conversely, the highly populated Detroit Metropolitan area has five House representatives. All told, the lower third of Michigan accounts for 10 of the state's 15 House members.

Current Michigan Senator Carl Levin (D) holds the record as Michigan's longest-serving U.S. Senator. He has been representing Michigan since 1979 and has won re-election five times. Prior to his re-election, Levin held many posts in Michigan, including assistant state attorney general and president of the Detroit City Council.

Michigan's longest-serving House member is Representative John Dingell (D), who has represented his suburban Detroit district since 1955. Prior to that, Dingell's father, John Dingell Sr. (D), represented the district. Dingell's own son, Chris, was elected a Michigan state senator. You might say that serving Michigan runs in the family!

Michigan's President

Gerald R. Ford, Jr. (1913–2006) is not always fondly remembered. He's known as the president who let Richard Nixon off the hook; as the president who withdrew the last troops from Vietnam; and as the guy who fell off the steps of Air Force One (and fell everywhere else, too). He's also known as the Unelected President, for he was never actually elected to either the Presidency or the Vice Presidency—he took the first after the resignation of Spiro Agnew and the second after the resignation of Nixon. Ford was the only person in history to have held both positions unelected.

None of this has stopped Michigan from embracing its hometown President. Ford was born in Nebraska but moved to Grand Rapids when he was still a toddler. He was originally named Leslie Lynch King, Jr., after his father, but when his mother moved to Michigan, she left King Sr. and married a paint salesman named Gerald Ford (no relation to Henry). They unofficially rechristened the toddler as Gerald Ford Jr., though it would be years before the renaming was made official.

Ford attended the University of Michigan at Ann Arbor, where he majored in economics and political science. He also majored in winning as part of U of M's football Wolverines. He became a hometown star on the gridiron, earning two national championships and a 1974 MVP nod. The Detroit Lions very nearly drafted him! Instead, Ford earned his law degree at Yale, served in World War II and then began practicing law in Grand Rapids. In 1949, he easily won election to the U.S. House of Representatives. Ford served the Grand Rapids district for 12 terms, until his appointment to vice president in 1973.

Today, the Gerald R. Ford Library stands in Ann Arbor, and his Presidential Museum is in Grand Rapids. It is located at 303 Pearl Street, includes such historic mementos as the Watergate burglary tools (presumably the Nixon Museum didn't want them), several of his wife Betty's gowns, the pistol whipped out by Lynette "Squeaky" Fromme before she was tackled by Secret Security agents, an apology letter from would-be Assassin #2, Sara Jane Moore, and the staircase that stood atop the U.S. Embassy in Saigon as the last Americans were famously photographed being airlifted out of town. When Ford died in late 2006, he was buried on the library grounds.

First Black Mayor

Detroit's first black mayor was the memorable, controversial Coleman Young (1918–97), who served five terms from 1974–93. Young was born in Alabama but moved to Detroit when he was young. He served as one of the famed Tuskegee Airmen in World War II and afterward worked as a civil rights leader and a labor activist. His political career began when he was elected to the Michigan State Senate (representing Detroit, of course).

Young's tenure as mayor was one of both ups and downs. He had some incredible successes, such as the building of Joe Louis Arena and the Renaissance Center, but he also had some spectacular controversies, including accusations of kickbacks (never proven) and a consistent animosity with the mostly-white suburbs. Through it all, Young remained himself, a vocal, outspoken, blunt man. He was especially noted for his plain way of stating things, often laced with profanities. Here are some memorable Young-isms (edited, as some of them really can't be printed otherwise):

"Swearing is an art form. You can express yourself much more exactly, much more succinctly, with properly used curse words."

"Racism is something like high blood pressure—the person that has it doesn't know he has it until he drops over with a g*d**n stroke."

"Some people say affirmative action is discrimination in reverse. You're d*** right. The only way to handle discrimination is to reverse it."

"You don't grow balls. Either you got 'em or you don't."

"That [jerk] Waldmeir followed me down to Jamaica. All I can say is, I wish that [jerk] had caught me. I'm mayor of nothing down there. It would be just two crazy Americans fighting in the alley."

LABOR OF LOVE

The State of Unions

If you're from Michigan, chances are you know someone who belongs to a labor union. For most of the 20th century, labor unions were a powerful force in Michigan politics. Detroit, "Union Town," was the center of that power, but union influence reached across the state. The most well-known union is the United Auto Workers, or UAW, and when a Michigander says "the Union" he's probably talking about it. There's also the International Brotherhood of Teamsters, or just "the Teamsters," which represents laborers, farmers, truckers and others; its most famous member is the long-gone Jimmy Hoffa. There are also smaller unions for every conceivable job, including miners, lumberjacks, typographers, printers, teachers and even public employees. The result has been higher wages, better working conditions and general economic improvement for Michigan.

The auto unions were also a driving force for the influx of immigrants in the 20th century. Over the past 100 years, Eastern Europeans, Scandinavians, Arabs, Turks, Belgians, Italians, Greeks, Hispanics and more have arrived in Michigan to seek a better life in unionized jobs. They have settled throughout the state, but especially around Detroit, creating a classic American melting pot of cultures.

Unfortunately, an unstable economy, a push towards global manufacturing and the deregulation of industry have all contributed to the decline of labor union power in the state. Although unions still hold influence, fewer Michiganders are employed in union jobs each year.

DID YOU  KNOW?

The United Auto Workers has modernized and expanded in recent decades. It is now the United Automobile, Aerospace and Agricultural Implement Workers of America, and it represents not only autoworkers, but also those who build airplanes, tractors and other large-scale manufactured goods. It's still known as the UAW, though, for obvious reasons—try saying "the UAAAIWA" three times fast!

Sitting Down on the Job

The United Auto Workers union first organized in 1935, but it took a Michigan labor strike to spark it into real action. The Flint Sit-down Strike of 1936–37 was part of an effort to force GM to collectively bargain with the UAW for worker's contracts. During the strike, employees occupied the Flint Fisher Body plants, and later a Chevrolet engine plant, effectively shutting down GM's production. Soon, other autoworkers began daylong strikes in support of the Flint sit-down (and a companion strike at the body plant in Cleveland), some of them marching through the streets to show their solidarity.

Meanwhile, UAW leaders fought the legal and political firestorm. A judge tried to end the strike but was exposed as a GM stockholder. The police raided the plants with tear gas but were turned back with fire hoses. Legislation was considered. But in the end, the workers won out; GM agreed to sign its first-ever national contract with the UAW.

DID YOU  KNOW?

Automotive production in Michigan ceased during World War II, when union workers and assembly lines were dedicated fully to the war effort. Nearly all of Michigan's auto plants were turned to the production of planes, jeeps and other wartime needs. The hundreds of thousands of vehicles that rolled off of the state's assembly lines were dubbed the "Arsenal of Democracy."

FINE ARTS

Michigan's Fine Art House

Art appreciation in Michigan begins at the Detroit Institute of Arts, the DIA, which stands on the corner of Woodward and Warren. The DIA began as an 1883 art loan exhibit that was so successful that the state approved the creation of a permanent Detroit Museum of Art. The DMA opened in 1888. It was an immediate success, and by 1896 it was attracting nearly 100,000 visitors a year. In the 1920s, the museum reorganized and changed its name to the Detroit Institute of Arts. It also changed locations, moving into its current home on Woodward Avenue. Today, the DIA is the fifth largest art museum in the U.S.

Notable Holdings:
Detroit Industry by Diego Rivera.
  Unveiled in 1933, this four-wall mural cycle uses as its subject the factory life of the average Detroit worker of the 1930s. It is notable for its multicultural depiction of autoworkers, as well as for its unique use of Christian imagery and female nudes (all of which caused controversy on its 1933 unveiling).

Chapel from Chateau de Lannoy.
  This exhibit features a 14th-century Gothic chapel that was transported to Detroit. It includes stunning stained-glass windows.

Judith and Her Maidservant with the Head of Holofernes, by Artemisia Gentileschi.
  This impressive post-Renaissance work by a female artist depicts the moments after the infamous Biblical beheading.

Self Portrait, by Vincent Van Gogh.
  This oft-reproduced portrait of the artist shows Van Gogh in a wide-brimmed sun hat.

The Nightmare, by Henry Fuseli.
This Romantic-era masterpiece is one of the most famous in the DIA. It features a dark depiction of one woman in the grip of her nightmares, personified by a squatting imp and a devilish, dark horse—literally a night mare—coming out of the shadows.

Video Flag X, by Nam June Paik.
Visitors enjoy staring at this unique work, which consists of 84 television sets, each flickering patterns of images that together create an American Flag.

Watson and the Shark, by John Singleton Copley.
The DIA holds one of three versions of this painting. Its gruesome subject matter, young Lord Watson being rescued from a shark attack, makes it a popular stop on museum tours.

City Spirit

Detroit was given one of its most enduring symbols in 1958, when artist Marshall Fredericks (1908–98) dedicated his 26-foot bronze statue outside of the city municipal buildings. The statue depicts a toga-clad man sitting cross-legged with both hands held out. The left hand holds a copper ball emitting rays, symbolizing God; the right hand holds a human couple, symbolizing family. Behind the statue, etched in concrete tiles beneath Detroit's symbol, is a verse from 2 Corinthians 3:17, "Now the Lord is that Spirit: and where the Spirit of the Lord is, there is liberty."

Because it is cast in bronze, it has, like the Statue of Liberty, developed a green patina, earning the statue the nickname "the Jolly Green Giant." But it has a far more important unofficial name, the *Spirit of Detroit*. It has become a city icon, appearing in books, on websites and in documentaries about Detroit.

In 1997, a local sports group decided to help the Spirit of Detroit better reflect the local zeitgeist by turning him into a Red Wings fan. They fashioned a Red Wings jersey out of 35 feet of red cloth and plenty of snap fasteners and dressed the Spirit in it. The jersey was a hit with local sports fans, and so the Spirit has been dressed in the jersey every year since as the Red Wings approach the playoff season. He's even expanded his wardrobe in recent years, at various times donning a Pistons jersey and even a Super Bowl XL jersey, when the game came to nearby Ford Field in 2006.

Haddon Sundblom

Sundblom (1899–1976), the son of Finnish immigrants, was born in and raised in Muskegon. He moved to Chicago to pursue a career in commercial art and eventually landed a job doing advertisements for Coca-Cola. His most famous works are his paintings of Santa Claus, which he produced for Coca-Cola beginning in 1931. His soft, warm style and jolly, grandfatherly Santa toting a bottle of classic Coke was a quick hit, and Coca-Cola kept coming back to Sundblom's Santa year after year. Sundblom produced more than 30 images, solidifying the image of a larger-than-life Claus in the mind of Americans. Today, his Coca-Cola Santas continue to appear on Coke cans and billboards during the Christmas season and have even been put on placemats, posters and ornaments.

DID YOU KNOW?

Despite popular belief, Sundblom and Coca-Cola did not invent Santa's red and white suit. Santa was dressing in red and white at least 20 years before Sundblom's first painting. Sundblom's version did, however, become the image of Santa that dominates popular culture today.

A Serious Comic Collection

Michigan State University houses one of the largest catalogs of comic books and comic art in the world. The Comic Art Collection has over 150,000 comic books in its archives, including many valuable and hard-to-find issues, both in print and on microfilm. They also have more than 1000 collections of newspaper comic strips, plus an array of books on the history, criticism and culture of the comic book.

LITERATURE

The Young Man and Waloon Lake

The great writer Ernest Hemingway (1899–1961) was born in Illinois but spent nearly every summer of his childhood fishing the waters of northern Michigan. His family owned a property called Windermere on Waloon Lake near Petosky. During the summers, Hemingway would often travel throughout the state, fishing for trout in lakes, streams and rivers. He would later say that his summers in Michigan were some of the best times in his life.

Hemingway's time in Michigan became the basis for many stories. One fishing trip to Fox River in 1920 became the basis for "Big Two-Hearted River"—named after an actual river in Michigan, though not the Fox (Hemmingway would later admit that he changed the name "because Big Two-Hearted River is poetry"). His time in Michigan also influenced such stories as "The Light of the World," "Wedding Day," "The Indians Moved Away" and "Summer People." In many of these Michigan-inspired stories, Hemingway's protagonist is an autobiographical character named Nick Adams.

MAGNIFICENT MICHIGAN Windermere is still owned by the Hemingway family and remains closed to visitors. That does not dissuade the Michigan Hemingway Society from boating past the lakefront property during its annual Hemingway conference. A boat ride on Wahoon Lake is a feature of its gatherings, and Windermere is a point of interest during the tour.

"By the shores of Gitche Gumee..."

Poet Henry Wordsworth Longfellow's (1807–82) epic poem *The Song of Hiawatha* was inspired by the Native Americans living around Lake Superior. Longfellow refers to the lake by the name *Gitche Gumee*, a corruption of the Ojibwe name *Gichigami*, "big water." Michigan later named the area Hiawatha National Forest.

Birth of a Playwright

Arthur Miller (1915–2005), though born in New York, forged strong ties to Michigan when he attended the University of Michigan from 1934 to 38. It was during his years at the U of M that Miller began writing plays, with his very first, *No Villain*, earning him a Hopwood writing scholarship. Miller kept his connection to the U of M his entire life, establishing scholarships of his own and even lending his name to the U of M's Arthur Miller Theatre.

Caldecott Winner

Chris Van Allsburg (1949–) has written and illustrated 17 children's books, the two best known being *The Polar Express* and *Jumanji*. He was born in Grand Rapids, where his grandfather ran a local creamery, and he later attended the University of Michigan.

Industry Scrutiny

Author Arthur Hailey (1920–2004), best known for novels such as *Runway Zero Eight*, *Hotel* and *The Evening News*, turned his intensely researched fiction towards Detroit in 1971. *Wheels* set itself among the boardrooms and factories of National Motors Corporation, a fictionalized company based heavily on Ford and GM. It was probably not a bestseller amongst Detroit-area car executives.

MUSIC

Motown

Motown began as a record label, but it has lent its name to an entire style and time period of American music. Motown helped define a generation of African-American musicians and continues to influence artists today.

The General

Berry Gordy (1929–) was the man most responsible for Motown's success. As a young man, Gordy trained as a boxer, served in the U.S. army, ran a jazz record store and worked the assembly line at a Lincoln-Mercury plant. He also wrote songs and eventually gave up his other pursuits to write full time. After scoring successes with songs like "Reet Petite" and "Lonely Teardrops," Gordy built a stable of local African-American singers and founded his own company, Tamla. It would soon change its name to Motown.

The Strategy

Motown's success came largely from Gordy's "Motown Sound," a carefully executed formula for controlling the feel of the music. Lyrics had to be catchy and written in the present tense. Choruses had to be short, easily remembered and often repeated. The music limited itself to a few chords, with melodies that were looped. Rhythms had to be steady and even. It has been said that the sound was more important than the singer, and Gordy even claimed that the sound, more than the singer, sold the record. He may have been right, for the Motown Sound led to phenomenal success. In the 1960s and '70s, Motown charted dozens of hits and made overnight stars out of its artists.

Gordy, ever the salesman, also made sure that the Motown Sound was designed to play well through car radios and transistor radios, both of which were experiencing increased popularity in the 1960s. These radios were low fidelity and required clean, simple mixes for better listening. To ensure that Motown music would sound good in the car, Gordy would play mixes through a car radio to test them before release.

The Troops

Although one could fill a book with the history of Motown's greatest (and some have), here is a quick rundown of the movement's most notable names:

Marvin Gaye (1939–84) was Motown's top-selling male solo artist and is best known for the songs "I Heard It Through the Grapevine" and "Let's Get It On."

Michael Jackson, (1958–) the King of Pop, found his way to Motown in 1969 as part of the Jackson 5. Gordy put everything into marketing young Jackson and his brothers, and turning them into a media sensation with such hits as "ABC" and "I'll Be There." Jackson also began his solo career with the label.

Gladys Knight, (1944–) with her group the Pips, recorded several notable hits with Motown, though the song she's best known for, "Midnight Train to Georgia," was recorded after the group left the label.

William "Smokey" Robinson, (1940–) Detroit native, met Gordy as a teenager while auditioning with the Matadors. Robinson went on to contribute much to the Motown sound. As the lead singer of the Miracles, his hits included "Shop Around" and "The Tears of a Clown." As a songwriter, he penned such recognizable hits as "My Girl" and "The Way You Do the Things You Do."

Mary Wells, (1943–92) had one hit, the immediately recognizable "My Guy."

Lionel Richie (1949–) sparked his career with Motown as lead singer of the Commodores, where he fronted such hits as "Easy," "Three Times a Lady" and "Brick House."

Stevie Wonder (1950–), born in Saginaw, scored his first hit with Motown at age 13, with "Fingertips (pt.2)." It was the beginning of a long and successful career as an influential singer/songwriter. He has recorded for the Motown label ever since, creating such groundbreaking albums as *Music of My Mind* and *Songs in the Key of Life*.

The original home of Motown Records was a converted two-house lot known as Hitsville U.S.A. Today, Hitsville continues to operate as the Motown Museum, which opened to the public in 1988. Visitors can see many of the original instruments and much of the equipment used to record songs at Hitsville as well as listen to some of the actual recordings.

Queen of Soul

Aretha Franklin (1942–) was born in Memphis, Tennessee, but grew up in Detroit. Where, in her father's church, she began her successful singing career. She has since become a hometown favorite in addition to being recognized as the "Queen of Soul" around the world for hits such as "Respect" and "I Knew You Were Waiting." Franklin has been inducted into the Michigan Women's Hall of Fame and came back to Detroit to sing for Super Bowl XXL in 2006.

DID YOU KNOW?

Despite rising to fame in the Detroit area at the same time as the Motown movement, Franklin never recorded with Motown Records.

Number One with a Bullet

If you asked any random Michigan resident to name the state's greatest homegrown rocker, chances are they would name Robert Clark "Bob" Seger (1945–). Seger, an Ann Arbor native, has been a Michigan mainstay for more than 40 years.

Seger's music career began in the early 1960s, first as a background singer with bands such as the Decibels, and then as front-man for two eponymous groups: Bob Seger and the Last Heard, and The Bob Seger System. He became popular mainly in the Detroit area and eventually established a dedicated following in southern Florida, but national fame eluded him.

It would take the formation of his third group, Bob Seger and the Silver Bullet Band, for Seger to gain national fame. Things got rolling with the 1975 album *Live Bullet* (recorded in Detroit's Cobo Hall), and the 1976 album *Night Moves* firmly established Seger on the national stage. The title track was not only a national hit but has since been declared one of the most influential songs in rock 'n' roll.

Seger has crafted a string of hits since "Night Moves." His music draws from his blue-collar Michigan roots; his is the music of long hours, cold highways and roadside bars full of quiet strangers. His well-known hits include "Against the Wind," "Hollywood Nights," "Shakedown" and "Like a Rock" (which has since become an anthem for Chevy trucks). His best-known song is "Old Time Rock 'n' Roll," which gained added fame when it was featured in the Tom Cruise movie *Risky Business*.

Like a Michigander

Though now seemingly British and Jewish, Madonna Louise Ciccone (1958–), better known simply as Madonna, began her life as a Michigan native and a Roman Catholic. She was born in Bay City, near Flint, and was raised in the Detroit suburb of Pontiac. Madonna's family was, like many Michigan families, part of the Detroit automotive industry; her father worked for Chrysler. After graduating from Rochester Adams High School, she spent two years on a dance scholarship at the University of Michigan.

Ultimately, Madonna moved on to bigger cities—New York, Los Angeles, London—and an even bigger music career, recording such hits as "Like a Virgin," "Like a Prayer" and "Vogue." It seems she has no love for her former home, though, as she once described her Bay City birthplace as "a smelly little town in Northern Michigan."

Motor City Madman

Bluegrass rock guitarist Ted Nugent (1948–), a.k.a. Gonzo, Terrible Ted, The Nuge and a dozen other nicknames, was born in Detroit and lived for many years in Jackson. His first band was called the Detroit Amboy Dukes. During his years in Michigan, he was well known as an extreme activist for hunter's rights. He even considered a run for governor, though the campaign never took shape.

Welcome to My Hometown

Legendary shock rocker Vincent "Alice Cooper" Furnier (1948–) is a Detroit native, even though he spent most of his childhood in Arizona. Cooper moved his fledgling act back to Detroit in 1970, where his wild stage performances became popular. Cooper has since credited the Motor City with helping him become the star he is today.

Eminem

Marshall Bruce Mathers III (1972–), known to the world as Eminem, was raised in the Detroit area, though he was born in Missouri. During his time in Michigan, Eminem lived a hard life. Reportedly, his family was poor and constantly moving, sometimes living with relatives or on the streets. He was discovered in Detroit by another notable local rap producer, Dr. Dre, and has since become one of the most famous rappers in the world. Eminem is recognized as an influential and innovative voice in modern music, though he is also criticized for his frequent use of drugs, sex and violence as subject matter. His life in Detroit was the inspiration for the 2002 film *8 Mile*.

ON THE AIR WAVES

Radio Stars

As a state known for its music, it's no wonder that Michigan has been home to a number of talented radio personalities.

What a Dummy!

Edgar Bergen (1903–78) was born in Chicago, IL, but grew up in Decatur. He is probably best remembered for his sidekick, the humorous dummy Charlie McCarthy, with whom Bergen co-hosted his radio show. Bergen's daughter Candice, was the star of the hit series *Murphy Brown* and more recently *Boston Legal*.

From the Front Lines

Charles Collingwood (1917–85) made his name as a war reporter in World War II, broadcasting from Normandy Beach on D-Day. He later reported from Vietnam, earning awards for his work. He was born in Three Rivers.

Ball Caller

William "Ernie" Harwell (1918–) was a Washington, GA, native, but his claim to fame is as the most familiar voice in all of Michigan. Called the "Voice of the Tigers," Harwell spent 42 years calling games for the hometown team. He still makes the occasional appearance on Detroit radio.

The Voice of Detroit

Joseph Priestly "J.P." McCarthy (1933–95) was a fixture on Detroit radio for 39 years, broadcasting for news station WJR. The New York, NY, native was so popular in Detroit that, after his untimely death from leukemia in 1995, local radio stations aired a simultaneous minute of silence.

Chart-Keeper

Casey Kasem (1932–), born in Detroit, is best known for his long-running American Top 40 radio program. Many don't know that he also provided the voice for loveable coward Shaggy in the Scooby-Doo cartoons.

Royal Radio

Esther Van Wagoner Tufty (1896–1986), nicknamed "the Duchess," was a pioneer of women in broadcasting. She is best known for her Tufty Topics radio show. The Duchess was a native of the Thumb area.

MEDIA AND ENTERTAINMENT

Michigan's Native Son

Though his actual birthplace was Athens, Georgia, Jeff Daniels (1955–) has become Michigan's most dedicated actor and a true Michigander.

Daniels grew up in Chelsea, where his family owns a lumber mill, and he attended Central Michigan University after finishing high school. He has gone on to a successful movie career, making his name as a versatile character actor and occasional leading man. His best-known films include *Terms of Endearment*, *Arachnophobia*, *The Purple Rose of Cairo* and *Gettysburg*.

Despite his success, Daniels has not forgotten Michigan. He still lives in Chelsea, where he has built a stage theatre, The Purple Rose, and founded a theatre company to perform there. He also wrote a play, *Escanaba In Da Moonlight*, which poked fun at Michigan's hunting culture. *Escanaba* premiered at the Purple Rose and was later turned into a movie, which was also filmed locally. Daniels has since written a sequel, *Escanaba in Love*.

 The Purple Rose Theatre Company is dedicated to performing plays written by Michiganders about life in Michigan and the Midwest. The company also keeps the price of tickets modest, so that more people can afford to attend the theatre.

Michigan Godfather

Francis Ford Coppola (1939–), best known for the *Godfather* and its sequels, was born in Detroit. His father, musician and composer Carmine Coppola, was first flutist for the Detroit Symphony Orchestra when Coppola was born. When Francis was two, the Coppolas moved out of Michigan.

Michael Moore

Polarizing documentary filmmaker and political activist Michael Moore was born in 1950 and raised in Flint, the town he later made famous with his documentary *Roger & Me.* Moore made the film after auto company General Motors, around which most of Flint's economy was based, began closing plants and laying off thousands of workers. *Roger & Me* documented how the closures hurt Flint and its suburbs, and also chronicled Moore's futile efforts to interview GM CEO Roger B. Smith.

The success of *Roger & Me* launched Moore into a series of increasingly successful (and often increasingly controversial) documentaries. In his film *Bowling for Columbine,* Moore returned to Michigan, interviewing members of the Michigan Militia and residents of Oscoda as part of a larger exploration of America's gun culture. It won the Academy Award for Best

Documentary Feature in 2002. His 2004 film, *Fahrenheit 9/11*, continued to tap local stories, telling the tale of local military mother Lila Lipscomb.

 Beginning in 2005, Moore has lent his support to the Traverse City Film Festival, which he helped found with writer Doug Stanton and photographer John Robert Williams. The festival provides new filmmakers who have not received wide distribution a venue to have their movies shown and promoted. It has been highly successful in its first two years, and plans are to continue the festival in the future.

Sam the Man and Buddy Bruce

Samuel Marshall "Sam" Raimi (1959–), director, producer and cult horror icon, began his life in the Detroit suburb of Royal Oak and was educated at Michigan State University. Parts of his first cult hit film, *The Evil Dead*, were filmed in Marshall, and the entire cast (all five of them!) were Michigan natives. The film (and its sequel, *The Evil Dead 2*) was widely noted for its over-the-top gore and sick humor. Raimi has since gone on to direct such films as *Darkman*, *A Simple Plan*, *For the Love of the Game*, *Spider-Man*, *Spider-Man 2* and *Spider-Man 3*.

Bruce Campbell (1958–), also a Royal Oak native, starred in each of Raimi's early films. While Raimi has gone on to become an A-list director, Campbell has settled firmly into the role of perennial B-list star, making such cult films as *Maniac Cop* and *Bubba Ho-Tep*. He still maintains his friendship with Raimi, and the director has given Campbell a cameo spot in many films.

LEADING MEN

Michigan has produced a fair share of dashing, notable leading men:

Vader's Voice

Rumbly-voiced actor James Earl Jones (1931–) was actually born in Mississippi but moved to Michigan at age five. He graduated from the University of Michigan and was also a member of the Michigan ROTC before going on to become the voice of both Darth Vader and CNN.

Built in Michigan
Lee Majors (1939–) is best known for playing the Six Million Dollar Man and the Fall Guy. He was born Harvey Lee Yeary in Wyandotte.

Walkabout

Terry O'Quinn (1952–) was born as Terrance Quinn in the village of Newbury. He later attended Central Michigan University. He has become a noted character actor, best known for playing John Locke on the series *Lost* and has appeared in *Star Trek*, *Alias*, *The West Wing* and *The X-Files*.

The Plan Man
Depending upon which generation you're from, you likely remember Dearborn native George Peppard (1928–94) best for either his breakout role in *Breakfast at Tiffany's,* or his turn as cigar-chomping John "Hannibal" Smith on *The A-Team*, where his most famous line was "I love it when a plan comes together."

Moustache Man
Tom Selleck (1945–) was born in Detroit but raised in California. He's best known as TV's *Magnum, P.I.*

He's the Sheriff

Tom Skerritt (1933–), a popular actor in both film and television, was born and raised in Detroit. He also attended Wayne State University. He's remembered for his role as Sheriff Jimmy Brock in *Picket Fences* and also has notable roles in such films as *Alien, Top Gun*, and *M*A*S*H**.

Dashing Lead

Robert Wagner (1930–) was born in Detroit before moving to Los Angeles at age seven. Older audiences best remember him as Alexander Mundy in *It Takes a Thief* or as Jonathan Hart in *Hart to Hart*, while younger audiences recognize him first as Number Two, Dr. Evil's right-hand man in the Austin Powers films.

LEADING LADIES

The following women all started out on Michigan's pleasant peninsulas:

Junior Detective
Television's *Veronica Mars*, Kristen Bell (1980–) was born in Detroit and raised in Royal Oak.

A Grand Actress

Ellen Burstyn (1932–) began life as Edna Rae Gillooly in Detroit. She has become a distinguished star of stage and screen, winning an Academy Award for *Alice Doesn't Live Here Anymore* in 1974. She is best known as distraught mother Chris McNeill in *The Exorcist*.

Unusual Comedienne
Sandra Bernhard (1955–) was born in Flint. She has is a multi-talented actress, author, and comedian, appearing on stage and screen. She's well known for her friendship with another Michigan girl, Madonna.

Never Mind!

Funny lady Gilda Radner (1946–89) was born and raised in Detroit before heading off to New York and *Saturday Night Live* fame. She went on to marry actor Gene Wilder before succumbing to cancer.

Multiple Award Winner
Actress and comedian Mary Jean "Lily" Tomlin (1939–) is a Detroit native. She attended Wayne State University before heading to Hollywood to star in such films as *Nashville* and *9 to 5*. She has since earned Tonys, Emmys and even a Grammy Award.

FILMED IN MICHIGAN

All of the following movies were filmed, in whole or in part, in Michigan:

8 Mile (2002)
61* (2000)
Action Jackson (1987)
American Pie 2 (2001)
Anatomy of a Murder (1959)
Aspen Extreme (1992)
Assignment Berlin (1981)
Below (2001)
The Betsy (1978)
Beverly Hills Cop (1984)
Beverly Hills Cop II (1987)
Blue Collar (1978)
Bowling for Columbine (2002)
Chameleon Street (1988)
Chasing Sleep (1999)
Cobb (1994)
Collision Course (1987)
Continental Divide (1981)
Crimewave (1983)
Crossing the Bridge (1993)
Detroit 9000 (1973)
Detroit Rock City (1999)
Die Hard II (1990)
Doctor Detroit (1983)
Driven (2000)
Escanaba in da Moonlight (2000)
The Evil Dead (1982)
The Evil Dead II (1987)
Flirting with Disaster (1995)
The Four Corners of Nowhere (1994)
Full Blast (1996)
Grosse Pointe Blank (1997)
Hard Ball (2000)
Hardcore (1979)
Hatred of a Minute (1995)
Hemmingway (1988)
Hoffa (1992)

In the Woods (1997)
The Island (2005)
Judicial Consent (1994)
Lunatics: A Love Story (1989)
Madonna: Truth or Dare (1991)
Midnight Run (1987)
Moontrap (1988)
Mosquito (1995)
MVP (2002)
Narc (2002)
One Room Castle (1993)
Only the Lonely (1991)
Polish Wedding (1997)
Prancer (1989)
Presumed Innocent (1990)
Rachel's Attic (1999)
Reach the Rock (1997)
Renaissance Man (1994)
Road to Perdition (2001)
The Rosary Murders (1986)
Roger & Me (1989)
Scarecrow (1973)
Singapore Harbor (1988)
Somewhere in Time (1980)
Standing in the Shadows
of Motown (2002)
Super Sucker (2002)
Tainted (1997)
Tanner '88 (1988)
This Time for Keeps (1946)
Tiger Town (1983)
Tough Enough (1983)
Transformers (2007)
True Romance (1993)
The Upside of Anger (2005)
Where the Boys Are (1960)
Zebrahead (1991)

Despite being set in Detroit, the 1989 sci-fi film *Robocop* was filmed in Dallas, Texas.

Everybody Loves a Parade

Each Thanksgiving, Detroit challenges New York to put on the best parade in the country. The America's Thanksgiving Day Parade marches down Woodward Avenue each "Turkey Day," a production full of local flavor and national talent. The theme of the parade is a storybook, and so most of the floats and balloons are children's stories such as *Little Red Riding Hood*, the *Wizard of Oz* and the *Very Hungry Caterpillar*. Each year, the parade ends with Santa Claus, who is given a key to the city. After 80 years, Santa must have quite a collection of them! The local parade is currently carried on Detroit's WDIV, which also happens to be the local NBC affiliate. For many years, NBC has carried the Macy's Parade on Thanksgiving morning, but in Detroit it is the America's Parade that airs live first; the Macy's Parade airs later in the day.

The parade is joined by two other Detroit Thanksgiving event traditions. The first is the black-tie Hob Nobble Gobble, which takes place the night before the parade. This celebrity and media event features games, dining and live performances at a cost of $350 or more per ticket. The second event is the annual Turkey Trot, a 10k run through Detroit's downtown that happens on Thanksgiving morning before the parade. The Trot has been happening for 25 years. More than 800 runners participated in the event in 2006. Both events are staged to support the America's Thanksgiving Day Parade.

One of the most unusual sights in the parade is the Fred Hill Briefcase Drill Team. This group of "precision businessmen" march the route in suits (and sometimes Santa hats), performing synchronized drills with their black briefcases. Parade-goers look forward to the team every year, and they're always a crowd favorite.

ARCHITECTURE

Mighty Mac

When your state is split in two, it should be expected that you'd spend some extraordinary time and effort to connect the halves. Thus it was with the Mackinac Bridge, Michigan's pride of suspension engineering and a nationally known symbol of the state. It spans the Straits of Mackinac between Mackinaw City in the Lower Peninsula, and St. Ignace in the Upper Peninsula.

Michiganders call the Mackinac Bridge the Mac, the Big Mac, the Mighty Mac and simply the Bridge. The two steel towers that hold the bridge stand 550 feet above the water and extend another 200 feet beneath it. The cable strung from the towers is 2 feet in diameter. Towers and cables support a surface that is only 54 feet wide but a lengthy 8614 feet from anchorage to anchorage (the points where the suspension cables are anchored) and a full 5 miles from shore to shore. At its highest, the bridge is nearly 200 feet above the water.

The bridge is so long and is surrounded by so much open water, that some people cannot even drive across it themselves. They find it uncomfortable, or just plain scary. The Mackinac Bridge Authority provides drivers for nervous travelers, free of charge. The Bridge Authority also provides a transport service for bicyclers and snowmobilers who wish to cross, though that service comes at a fee (currently around $10).

Building the Bridge

Before they built the Mac, there were only two ways to cross the Straits of Mackinac: swimming or boating…and swimming wasn't a very realistic option. Instead, ferries were the vehicles of choice. They ran regularly between peninsulas, carting people, cars and even livestock. Hunting season was a particularly trying time to cross the Straits; cars would line up and wait for 24 hours to get a ferry ride.

Talk of a bridge went on for decades before the Mighty Mac project got underway. No project ever seemed to take, and the state legislature was put off by the costs of such a project. Finally, in 1932, the Mackinac Bridge Authority was created to bring a bridge to completion. The entire project was funded by the sale of bonds at a total cost of $100 million dollars—it would take until 1986 to retire the lot. Three-hundred-and-fifty engineers helped to design the bridge, under the direction of Dr. David Stineman. More than 10,000 people contributed to the project, including sailors, metal smiths, construction workers, divers and a host of others. The actual construction took three years.

The Mackinac Bridge opened on November 1, 1957 (just in time for hunting season). The first cars to drive across it carried Governor G. Mennen Williams and the heads of the Mackinac Bridge Authority.

 Driving is the only way to cross the Mac, except on Labor Day, when two of the Mac's four lanes are closed for the Bridge Walk. On Labor Day in 1958, Governor Williams began the tradition with a mere 68 participants. It has since grown to an average of 50–60,000 participants. The governor of Michigan always heads the walk, except once, in 1992, when President George H.W. Bush led the walk in an attempt to generate state support for his re-election. It didn't work.

 Michigan originally became home to the world's largest shore-to-shore suspension bridge in 1929 when the Ambassador Bridge was built between Detroit and Windsor, Ontario. In 1957, the Ambassador was surpassed by the Mackinac Bridge, which itself was declared the longest shore-to-shore. Today, the Mighty Mac's shore-to-shore length ranks third in the world but is still longest in the Western Hemisphere.

DID YOU  KNOW?

In June 1973, an Amish family crossed the Mac in a horse and buggy, the first on record to do so. It took them an hour to cross.

Michigan's Lighthouses

With four lakes and an important seaway, it's no surprise that Michigan boasts many impressive lighthouses—116 of them, dotting the coastline from Detroit and Benton Harbor in the Lower Peninsula, all the way to Manitou Island at the very tip of the Upper Peninsula. Many of the lighthouses are still in operation, guiding the ever-present boat traffic on the Great Lakes. Others have been refurbished into museums or private homes, and three even serve as bed and breakfasts. A number are simply closed and are in a state of disrepair. Here are some notable lighthouses:

Fort Gratiot Light—located near Port Huron's Blue Water Bridge, it's the oldest lighthouse in Michigan. It was built in 1825.

Grand Traverse Light—also known as the "Northport Light," this no-longer-functioning lighthouse has been turned into a lighthouse museum.

William Livingston Memorial Light—on Belle Isle in the Detroit River it is the only one in America made of marble. It is dedicated to a former president of the Lake Carrier's Association, a lake trading organization.

Mackinac Round Island Light—squat and made of brick it is probably the most-viewed in the state. It stands near the popular tourist destination Mackinac Island and is a favorite for shutterbugs. No visitors are allowed.

St. Joseph North Pier Lights—a pair that represents one of the only still-operating pier light systems in Michigan. This was also the site of the first lighthouse on lake Michigan, though the original structure no longer stands.

White Shoal Light—built in 1910, it is unique for its bright red-and-white-spiral paintjob, the only one like it on the Great Lakes. The stripes make the lighthouse stand out against the lake and sky, aiding ships in navigating.

Whitefish Point Light—it is not the most attractive light in Michigan because it is surrounded by iron support scaffolding. But it was one of the first locations on Lake Superior to have a lighthouse (the original building was destroyed). The Whitefish Light is also attached to the Great Lakes Shipwreck Museum, making it a frequent tourist destination.

Detroit Renaissance

No building defines the Detroit skyline like the Renaissance Center. Its Renaissance Tower, built in the early 1970s, took 7000 workers more than two years to complete. The "RenCen," as locals refer to it, houses the municipal offices of the city of Detroit, General Motors' international headquarters and many private tenements, and the central tower serves as a Marriott hotel, the tallest in the Western hemisphere. The Renaissance Center has also become an icon of the city, serving as a representative shot of Detroit in books, magazines and websites.

The Capitol Building

It's a national trend to house state government offices in buildings modeled on the U.S. National Capitol Building, and Michigan was one of the first to do so. Designed by Elijah E. Myers and completed in 1879, the State Capitol building features a spired dome and Romanesque architecture. Its interior is decorated in a style known as Victorian painted decorative art—an elaborate and colorful style that combines decorative furniture and fixture painting with plenty of faux wall techniques. First-time visitors are always awed by the Capitol's décor, which seems to inhabit every nook and cranny of the place—there's no such thing as a boring view! The building's interior artistry earned it a National Historic Landmark designation on October 7, 1992.

DID YOU KNOW?

The original Michigan capital was Detroit. After the War of 1812, state leaders feared invasion by British troops, who were stationed across the river in Windsor. They voted to move the capital to the more defensible Lansing in 1847.

INVENTORS AND INVENTIONS

Thomas Edison

Though born in Milan, OH, famed inventor Thomas Alva Edison (1847–1931) spent most of his childhood years in Port Huron. Edison was considered a problem child at the time, but the city has since come to embrace its former citizen. Residents have named an elementary school for him and opened up a museum at the train depot where he worked as a young man. As an adult, Edison forged close ties with another great Michigan inventor, Henry Ford. Ford founded the Edison Electric Institute in honor of his friend, which now in turn runs the Dearborn-based Henry Ford Museum.

DID YOU  KNOW?

Edison, a prolific inventor, held 1097 patents in his lifetime and was known as "the Wizard of Menlo Park.," His biggest invention was the incandescent light bulb, followed closely by the phonograph, a practical electric grid, the motion picture camera and many other inventions without which our lives wouldn't be the same.

The Typewriter
The first typewriter was patented in Michigan by William Austin Burt, in 1829. Called a "typeographer," the cumbersome wooden box worked by pressing the letter key directly down onto the paper.

Spiral-Sliced Ham

If you've ever sat down for a holiday dinner of spiral-sliced ham, you have a Michigander to thank: Harry J. Hoenselaar, inventor of the spiral slicer. Hoenselaar, a Detroit area native, spent nearly 25 years perfecting the machine in his basement before obtaining the patent in 1949. And it was only after another eight years of trying to sell his invention that a frustrated Hoenselaar decided to go into business for himself. He took out a second mortgage on his house and used the cash to open up the first HoneyBaked Ham Co. store in Detroit.

Hoenselaar didn't stop with cutting the ham. He also perfected a process for curing and cooking ham, as well as for creating the sweet honey glaze that HoneyBaked Ham Co. is named for. Between the slicer and the cooking process, Hoenselaar and his family were able to grow HoneyBaked Ham Co. into a nationwide business. Hoenselaar's original patent for the spiral slicer expired in 1980, and today spiral-sliced ham is as common as sliced bacon.

The Real McCoy

Elijah McCoy (1843–1929) was the son of escaped slaves who had fled to Canada via the Underground Railroad. McCoy, who spent much of his youth in Detroit and studied mechanical engineering in Europe, was a crafty inventor. While working for the Michigan Central Railroad, McCoy invented a self-oiling bearing lubrication system that revolutionized the way locomotives functioned. It saved companies both time and money, and thus was an instant success.

Because success breeds imitation, others tried to recreate the new lubricator. Legend tells us that these imitators weren't quite up to snuff, though, so buyers wanting the original, reliable McCoy lubricator had to be sure and ask for "the real McCoy" when ordering parts. With time, the term "real McCoy" came to be used a general phrase for those seeking the genuine article.

The Carpet Sweeper

Battle Creek inventor Melville Bissell (1843–89) invented the carpet sweeper in 1876 at the request of his wife Anna. She was frustrated by sawdust in her carpets, which she could never sweep out with a straw broom. Bissell put his head to the task and came up with the design for the first carpet sweeper. His design was so successful that he went into business selling them, and Bissell Inc. produces sweepers and other carpet cleaners to this day.

Kitty Litter

It was a Cassopolis man, Edward Lowe, who gave millions of cats a place to go (and millions of kids an extra chore). Before Lowe came along, indoor cats went in boxes full of sawdust, sand or fireplace soot, which worked fine for the cat but left dusty paw prints all over the house. Lowe, an industrial absorbents salesman, hit upon using fuller's earth, a kind of clay that was sold for industrial oil and odor control. The idea quickly caught on, and Lowe went into business selling his kitty litter full time.

DID YOU  KNOW?

A litter box is necessary for cats because cats instinctively bury their feces to cover the scent from predators. In the wild, all the cats in a destruction (yes, that's what a group of wild cats is called) display such behavior—except for the dominant male, that is. The lead male proudly marks his territory with his leavings. When cat owners have a problem with their cat "going" on floors, sofas or tabletops, it's usually because the cat is displaying dominant behavior.

NOTABLE NAMES IN SCIENCE

Michiganders in Space

Michigan has contributed a number of fine astronauts to NASA's space program. Roger Chaffee (1935–67) was going to be the first Michigander in space. He was selected as one of the first pilots for the ambitious Apollo program, which eventually took man to the Moon. Sadly, Chaffee and his fellow astronauts burned to death aboard Apollo I during a botched test launch. Chaffee was born in Grand Rapids, where the town has named a planetarium in his honor.

Two other Michigan astronauts served in the Apollo program. James McDivitt (1929–), from Jackson, became the first Michigander in space when he commanded the Apollo 7 mission. He also served as a Gemini pilot during the first American space-walk. Fellow Jackson astronaut Al Worden (1932–) commanded

Apollo 15, one of America's six lunar visits; though Worden stayed in orbit while his fellow astronauts landed, he is technically the first (and, to date, only) Michigander to visit the Moon.

Cass City astronaut Brewster Shaw (1945–) participated in the Space Shuttle program in the 1980s. He flew three missions, twice with Columbia and once with Atlantis. Later, Shaw served as Operations Manager at Kennedy Space Center.

But is it Friable?

The Upjohn Company was for many years a premium name in medicine. Its founder, Dr. William Erastus Upjohn (1853–1932) was a graduate of the University of Michigan and spent a decade in Hastings as a doctor. He was particularly interested in finding a better way to deliver medicine, which in those days usually came in a foul-tasting syrup or a bitter, hard-to-digest pill. In 1885, Upjohn finally hit upon a formula for a "friable" pill— that is, a pill that dissolved easily, thus making it far more effective. The invention was an instant success, and soon the Upjohn Pill and Granule Company opened in Kalamazoo. The company was purchased by Phamacia, and that company has since been bought by Pfizer. Upjohn's friable pill is still used today.

Monopoly-buster

Herbert Henry Dow (1866–1930) put the town of Midland on the map when he opened up his Dow Chemical Company there in 1897. The earth beneath Midland was steeped in bromine, and Dow developed a way to extract it with relative ease and low cost. But there was a problem: the Germans held a virtual worldwide monopoly on bromine. They didn't approve of some upstart American trying to undermine them, so they flooded the American market with cheap bromine, attempting to undercut Dow and run him out of business.

Dow didn't kowtow. Instead, he secretly bought all of their super-cheap bromine, repackaged it, priced it just below the normal German price and began to undercut the Germans in the

European market. At one point, Dow was making a 16.5-cent profit on every pound of German bromine he purchased—nearly double the price he was paying for it! The Germans not only failed to shut Dow down, but they allowed him to gain a foothold in the European bromine market. Dow single-handedly broke the German monopoly on bromine, making him forever a hero of free market capitalists.

 Today, Dow has moved on from bromine extraction and has become a worldwide leader in plastics, chemicals and agricultural products. It is the second largest chemical manufacturer in the world.

Nuclear Power

Michigan is one of 31 states with nuclear power plants. There are three currently operating in the state: the Cook Energy Center in Bridgman, across Lake Michigan from Chicago; the Palisades Nuclear Plant in South Haven, just 40 miles north of the Cook Energy Center; and the Enrico Fermi Nuclear Generating Station, or Fermi II, in Monroe, south of Detroit. In total, they generate about 30-million kilowatt hours of energy a year.

A fourth plant, Big Rock Point in Charlevoix, was shut down in 1997 after 35 years of operation, because it was deemed too costly to upgrade. A fifth nuclear plant was begun in Midland, but public concerns about nuclear power in the early 1980s forced designers to convert it to a conventional power plant.

There has been one near-disaster at Michigan's nuclear plants. In October 1966, the original Fermi Station, Fermi I, approached a partial meltdown of its nuclear core after a small but vital part fractured. Though some claim that Michigan "almost lost Detroit" that night, any nuclear radiation was contained in the reactor core and posed no actual danger to the area. The Fermi I generator has since been replaced by the more modern Fermi II.

LIFE OF CRIME

Michigan's Prisons

Michigan operates 43 prisons as well as 10 corrections camps for minimum offenders. In 2004, there were 48,883 prisoners in the system, costing an average of $28,743 per inmate to feed, clothe and house. Both the sheer size of the prison population and the cost of incarcerating the prisoners have become big issues in recent years as Michigan struggles against a lagging economy. It is possible that in the near future, a significant number of these prisoners could be released (all considered "low-risk" releases, like those convicted for drug possession) or that one or more of Michigan's prisons could be shut down.

Devil's Night

What are you doing the night before Halloween? If you're in Michigan, and you're a teenager, you may be participating in Devil's Night. October 30 has always been a night for pranks, such as soaping car windows, tossing toilet paper into trees and over houses (known locally as "tee-peeing"), or lighting a paper bag full of doggie doo on a hated neighbor's porch (no, really, it's funny—they always try to stomp the flame out with their shoe). Tipping outhouses used to be a popular Devil's Night prank, too, though the practice has all but vanished as the outhouses themselves have disappeared.

In the 1970s, though, this state tradition took a wicked turn in economically depressed Detroit. With many of its citizens having fled to homes in the suburbs and many of the rest struggling to make ends meet, a darker, uglier Devil's Night emerged. The biggest problem was fire. Abandoned cars and buildings littering nearly every street in the city made perfect targets for vandals. Occupied homes and businesses were sometimes hit as well. And when buildings were not burned down, residents sometimes found their windows smashed and their belongings looted. Police and firefighters could not keep up with the Devil's Night destruction.

Things came to a head in 1984, when arsonists set a record 810 fires over a three-night period. The next year, Detroit implemented an anti-arson effort, using police, firefighters and volunteers to patrol the streets and keep an eye on high-risk areas. They labeled their effort Angel's Night and encouraged locals to use that name as well. Although the name hasn't caught on, the effort has; every year the anti-arson watch continues, and since 1985, the number of arsons occurring on Devil's Night has dropped significantly.

MALICIOUS MICHIGANDERS

Missing Teamster

The disappearance of Union boss Jimmy Hoffa (1913–?)in Michigan in 1975 initiated a string of rumors and legends that only the best unsolved crimes can produce. Hoffa was at one time the president of the International Brotherhood of Teamsters as well as a vocal politician. A bribery conviction and jail time had forced him out of both positions, but he was rumored to be planning a return to politics. He was also said to be poised to "blow the whistle" on certain mob connections within the Teamsters. On July 30, Hoffa left his home to meet a "contact" (possibly a mobster) at a restaurant in Bloomfield Hills. He was never seen again.

Hoffa was legally declared dead in 1982, but to this day his body has never been found. Many believe his remains were disposed of locally—in a gravel pit in Highland, beneath a concrete garage in Cadillac, dumped into the Detroit River, even crushed into a car compactor in Hamtramck. More fanciful legends claim, amongst other things, that Hoffa was taken to New Jersey and dumped into the concrete foundations of Giants Stadium. As recently as 2006, the FBI spent two weeks on a horse farm in Milford, tearing down a barn and digging up the ground in search of Hoffa's remains. They came up empty-handed, causing conspiracy theorists everywhere to sigh with relief.

The Unabomber is a Math Genius?

It's true: the Unabomber, Ted Kaczynski, was an outstanding mathematician at the University of Michigan. He earned both a Master's degree and a Ph. D. in mathematics over a five-year period and even taught classes there. He was considered a math genius, impressing both his professors and his peers…

… and he hated every minute of it. Kaczynski describes his time in Michigan as "the most miserable years of my life" and claims that he received almost no quality education at U of M. Criminologists think that it was during his years in Ann Arbor that Kaczynski developed his bombing psychosis. Perhaps not surprisingly, Kaczynski's favorite targets as the Unabomber were universities, including the University of Michigan.

DID YOU KNOW?

The name "Unabomber" was born out of Kaczynski's taste for college targets. The original FBI codename for his crimes was UNABOM, which stood for "University and Airline Bomber."

Three Bullets

Mob ties were also behind the killing of Albion state senator
Warren G. Hooper. Hooper was a corrupt politician who had
confessed to taking bribes and was about to "name names" in
court. Before he could testify, however, he was gunned down
in his car on January 11, 1945. The resulting investigation and
trial became a national media sensation. Officially, the case
remains unsolved. Unofficially, crime historians have found con-
vincing evidence that Hooper's own boss in the Michigan
Republican Party may have ordered his murder to prevent
Hooper from naming him at the trial.

Murder at the Lumberjack Tavern

In 1952, army Lieutenant Coleman A. Peterson entered the
Lumberjack Tavern in Big Bay and shot the bar owner, Mike
Chenoweth. After Chenoweth went down, Peterson leaned over
the bar and emptied his gun into the body. During the trial that
followed, Peterson admitted to the killing but claimed that he
killed Chenoweth for raping his wife. Questions were raised
about the claim, but in the end, Peterson was found not guilty
by reason of insanity. The trial itself was newsworthy locally but
was not a national sensation. That would have to wait until the
defense attorney for the trial fictionalized the case into a best-
selling novel.

Anatomy of a Murder

John D. Voelker (1903–91), a.k.a. Robert Travers, was born in
Ishpeming. He had a career as both a Michigan lawyer and
judge in addition to publishing fictional stories based on his
courtroom experiences. His most famous novel is *Anatomy of
a Murder* in which he fictionalized the Big Bay Lumberjack
Tavern murder trial. The book became an international bestseller, the biggest of Voelker's career. He was praised for his
realistic portrayal of courtroom procedure and his legalistic

insight—neither one difficult for a practicing attorney who had personally defended the case on which the story was based.

The book was turned into a movie staring Jimmy Stewart in the role of Paul Biegler (the fictionalized Voelker). Like the book, the film was an immediate success. It was notable for its open discussion of the details of the case, including rape, infidelity and women's undergarments—topics commonly "talked around" in films of the day. *Anatomy of a Murder* was filmed in and around Big Bay and Ishpeming, a fact that the towns tout today to draw tourists.

TEAM PLAYERS

We Do It All!

What sport isn't popular in Michigan? The state has professional representation in every major league sport in America, nearly all centered on Detroit. Why are they all in Detroit? Probably because Detroit is the only city with a population large enough to support such teams and the only area that has built professional-level facilities to house them.

Below is a complete listing of Michigan's professional teams and the leagues in which they play.

Detroit Fury	Arena Football League
Detroit Lions	National Football League
Detroit Pistons	National Basketball Association
Detroit Red Wings	National Hockey League
Detroit Shock	Women's National Basketball Assn.
Detroit Tigers	Major League Baseball
Grand Rapids Rampage	Arena Football League

DID YOU KNOW?

The U.P. houses a large number of "Packer Backers," fans of the Green Bay Packers football team. They justify this by pointing out that, for many of them, Green Bay is much closer than Detroit!

What's In a Name?

Modern teams like the Shock and the Fury have their names chosen by savvy marketers, but Detroit's older teams gained their monikers in more interesting ways.

Detroit Tigers

The Tigers took their name from a prominent Michigan military and social group, the Detroit Light Guard. The Light Guard was known informally as "the Tigers," and also used a tiger-head logo throughout the late 19th century. The group officially granted its name and logo to the team in 1901. Before then, baseball teams in Detroit were known variously as Detroit, the Detroits and the Wolverines.

Detroit Lions
The Lions were given their name in 1934 when they moved from Portsmouth (where they were the Spartans). The lion is "king of the jungle," and the team's new owner, George A. Richards, hoped the team would be king of the league. At least in the short term, he got his wish—the Lions dominated the league in the 1940s and 1950s.

Detroit Red Wings
Team owner James Norris adapted the Red Wings name and winged tire logo from the Montreal Amateur Athletic Association (MAAA) in 1932. The MAAA, which originated as a cycling club, used a winged bicycle wheel as its logo and often used the nickname "the Winged Wheelers" for its sports teams. Norris,

who had been a member of the MAAA hockey team, simply changed the wheel into an automobile wheel and called his team the Red Wings. Prior to that, the Red Wings had been called both the Falcons and the Cougars.

Detroit Pistons

Fort Wayne, IN, businessman Fred Zollner owned a piston-making factory, so when he formed a basketball team, he simply named it after his product. The result was the Fort Wayne Zollner Pistons, whose original mascot was a basketball player made out of pistons. By the time the team moved to Detroit, they dropped the "Zollner" (and the mascot) but kept the "Pistons," which fit the car-connected Motor City.

NOTABLE ATHLETES

Ty Cobb

Tyrus Raymond Cobb (1886–1961), "The Georgia Peach," played with the Detroit Tigers for 21 years, from 1905 to 1926. During his time with the team, he racked up an impressive list of accomplishments, some of which have yet to be surpassed, including a .367 lifetime batting average and touching 16 bases in a single American League game.

On the field, Cobb is credited with single-handedly making the Tigers into a notable ball club. He made an immediate impact on the game, winning the Tigers their first American League pennant in 1907 and taking them to the World Series in 1907, 1908 and 1909. He remained their star player throughout the next 15 years before retiring in 1926.

Off the field, Cobb was known for his high temper and outspoken opinions. He often got into fights and shouting matches with opponents, teammates and even fans. On one occasion, he attacked an injured autoworker in the middle of a game after the man heckled Cobb. When onlookers pointed out that Cobb was beating on a man with no hands (the heckler had lost all of one hand and part of the other in an accident), Cobb famously replied, "I don't care if he has no feet!" The event nearly led to Cobb's permanent suspension from the league.

George "The Gipper" Gipp

Born in the Upper Peninsula town of Laurium, "The Gipper" (1895–1920) is best known for his famous last words. Gipp made a name for himself playing for Notre Dame great Knute Rockne; during his time with the team, Gipp set many records. Sadly, he contracted fatal pneumonia in 1920. Gipp, on his death bed, famously (and possibly apocryphally) told coach Rockne, "Some time, Rock, when the team is up against it, when things are wrong and the breaks are beating the boys, tell them to go in there with all they've got and win just one for the Gipper." Gipp died soon after, but Rockne remembered his request eight years later, when he delivered the stirring message to the 1928 Notre Dame team just before they took on the undefeated Army team. The story did the trick. They did, indeed, "win one for the Gipper."

DID YOU  KNOW?

Former President Ronald Reagan played George Gipp in *The Knute Rockne Story* and uttered the famous last words onscreen. He later adopted both the phrase and the nickname to help fuel his presidential campaign.

Joe Louis

Known as "The Brown Bomber," Joe Louis Barrow (1914–81) grew up in Detroit after being born in Alabama. He began training as a boxer at age 16, and became simply "Joe Louis" when, during an amateur fight, he couldn't fit his whole name on an entry form. He became a boxing phenomenon, successfully defending the heavyweight boxing title 25 times and becoming a legend in his own time. Louis lived for many years in the Detroit area, before moving on to Chicago and Los Angeles.

Detroit has honored Lewis by building the Joe Louis Arena, a 20,000-seat sports complex. Joe Louis Arena currently serves as the home of the Detroit Red Wings.

Gordie Howe

Canadian-born Gordie Howe (1928–) first tried out for the New York Rangers at age 14 in 1942, but he was rejected. He tried out for the Red Wings a year later, where he impressed team owner Jack Adams as a "switch shooter" who could score from either side of the net. After some development, Howe joined the Red Wings in 1946. His arrival marked the beginning of the Red Wings' "Golden Age." Over the next decade, he helped lead the Wings to four Stanley Cup victories.

In his 25 years with the Red Wings, Howe won the Hart Trophy for MVP 6 times and the Art Ross Trophy for leading scorer 6 times. He was named to the All-Star First Team 12 times and was inducted to the Hockey Hall of Fame in 1972, a mere year after he left the Red Wings.

Joe Schmidt

Linebacker Joe Schmidt (1932–) had a stellar college career with the University of Pittsburgh. After college, it was his dream to play for his hometown Pittsburgh Steelers, but the Detroit Lions drafted him instead in 1953. It turned out to be a career-making move for Schmidt. As part of the all-star Lions of the 1950s, he became a 4-time Lions MVP and a 10-time Pro Bowler. He was noted for his speed, his power and his uncanny knack for "reading" the opposing team. Schmidt became so adept that when he retired from play, he was immediately made assistant coach. He later became the Lions' head coach.

Schmidt is best known as the player who perfected the role of middle linebacker. The position began to develop in the 1950s to counter changes to NFL offenses, which were opening gaps in their front lines to allow for more passing. Schmidt perfected the counter-strategy, forcing opposing offensive lines to plug their holes or offer their quarterbacks up for sacking. His pioneering play style in the new position helped earn him a spot in the Pro Football Hall of Fame.

Bobby Layne

Texas native and Longhorn alumni Bobby Layne (1926–86) came to the Detroit Lions in 1950 with an already impressive record: star college quarterback, four-time All Southwest Conference and two-time Heisman nominee. He brought a level of skill to the Lions that the team had never seen, launching them to the top of the NFL. During his eight years with the team, the Lions won three National Championships—the last three that the Lions have won to this day. He was not only a great athlete, but he was also a noted team leader. In the end, his on-the-field prowess with the Lions and later with the Pittsburgh Steelers earned Layne a spot in the Pro Football Hall of Fame.

 Layne was a phenomenal player, so it came as some surprise when he was traded away in 1958. Most surprised may have been Layne himself, who, according to local legend, laid a curse on the team when he was traded. Layne uttered

the threat, "The Lions won't win for 50 years!" as he was leaving town for Pittsburgh. Although not every Michigander believes in curses, there is no denying that the Lions have not won an NFL Championship since Layne's departure, and in fact have only won a single playoff game. The "curse," if it exists, is set to end in 2008…not a moment too soon for desperate Lions fans.

Earvin "Magic" Johnson

This huge hoops star was born and raised in East Lansing. While playing for Lansing Everett high school, Earvin Johnson (1959–) was named Associated Press and United Press All-State three years in a row. It was at this time that a local sports writer coined the nickname "Magic" to describe Johnson's talent. Johnson attended Michigan State University, where his roster of achievements included two All-Americas and an NCAA championship. His college play was so amazing that he was a first-round pick in the 1979 NBA Draft and went on to a successful career with the Los Angeles Lakers.

Johnson had a heck of a career in L.A., so great that he's never really come back to Michigan. After retirement, when he decided to open up a string of movie theatres, he chose not to bring the chain to the state.

Steve Yzerman

Steve Yzerman (1965–), a native of British Columbia, Canada, was drafted by the Detroit Red Wings in 1983. He was an immediate success, setting team rookie records and being declared Rookie of the Year. In the 23 years that followed, Yzerman became "The Captain," leading the Wings to two Stanley Cups and becoming a true Michigan hero. When Yzerman retired in 2006, he ranked as the sixth greatest scorer in NHL history. His number 19 jersey was quickly retired and hung with honor from the ceiling of the Joe Louis Arena.

Isiah Thomas

Detroit Pistons fans fondly remember Isiah Thomas (1961–), who was small of stature compared to his teammates, but who was a big playmaker with a big personality. Chicago native Thomas helped lead the Indiana Hoosiers to two NCAA titles before joining the Pistons in 1981. In his time with Detroit, Thomas earned two All-Star Game MVP awards, an NBA Finals MVP award and two championship rings (in 1989 and 1990). He is often best remembered for scoring a record 25 points in a single quarter during a 1988 playoff game—a feat he accomplished on a severely sprained ankle. Thomas was never the explosive player that some larger NBA stars have been, but his consistent excellence marked him forever as a Pistons great.

Dennis Rodman

Dennis Rodman (1961–) will probably be best remembered for his time with the Chicago Bulls, his celebrity shenanigans and his laughable acting career, but he began his rise to fame in Detroit. Drafted in 1986, Rodman helped the Pistons through their "Bad Boy" years, earning back-to-back Defensive Player of the Year awards in 1989 and 1990. His nickname, "the Worm," had nothing to do with his play style; his mother gave him the name as a child because he couldn't sit still.

NOTABLE MOMENTS

Bless You Boys!

Things had been glum for the Detroit Tigers for nearly 20 years when the team unexpectedly began its 1984 season with a 35–3 record. No one expected it; the team had not made any major trades nor signed any significant talents in the past year, but there the Tigers sat at the top of the league. Suddenly excited, the fans began expecting big things of their team. The Tigers delivered, scoring a franchise-record 104 wins in the regular season under the command of George "Sparky" Anderson and featuring such players as Kirk Gibson, Lou Whitaker and Alan Trammell.

By the time they began the playoffs, the Tigers were a Motor City phenomenon. They were dubbed the "Bless You Boys" by local media, a name the city embraced. T-shirts and pennants bore the name. People began to shout the slogan during games. A local band even recorded a song with that title, celebrating the team's winning season.

The Tigers dominated the playoffs that year. They swept the Kansas City Royals in three games and then won the World Series against the San Diego Padres in five games. Their whirlwind season and dominating playoff run have earned them a spot in the record books as only the third team in MLB history to lead an entire season and subsequently go on to win the World Series.

Bad Boys

The world loved to hate the 1989–90 Detroit Pistons. The team sported a line up of hard, fast, physical players whom many accused of playing dirty. Dennis Rodman, Mark Aguire, John Salley, Bill Lambier and Vinnie Johnson were amongst those dubbed "Bad Boys" by the media. The players did not complain; in fact they embraced the name, even going so far as to practice in black jerseys with skulls on the front.

On the court, the Bad Boys dominated. In the 1988–89 season, they won 63 games, a franchise record. They shut out their first two finals opponents, defeated Chicago in six games and then proceeded to sweep the L.A. Lakers to win the championship. The Pistons repeated in 1989–90, though with fewer wins and a less dominant playoff performance—it took them 5 games to beat the Portland Trail Blazers for the championship.

Paper Lions

Michigan football fans have long suffered the mediocre record of their hometown Lions. The team saw its "Golden Age" in the 1950s with three NFL championship wins and players such as Bobby Layne and Joe Schmidt controlling the ball. Since being purchased by the Ford family in 1964, however, the Lions have experienced a 47-year dry spell that has left fans dispirited and often cynical. Low points since 1964 include the following:

☛ They have a 274–365 losing record.

☛ They have won only a single playoff game—in 1991.

☛ They have never played in a Super Bowl.

☛ In 1990, they drafted quarterback Andre Ware, dubbed the "biggest Heisman flop of all time."

☛ Between 2001 and 2003, they became the first NFL team to go three seasons without a road victory.

☛ In 2005, angry fans staged a protest against current team president Matt Millen, under whom the Lions have posted the worst winning percentage in the NFL.

Every Thanksgiving, between the America's Thanksgiving Day Parade and a fine turkey dinner, Michiganders gather in front of the television for some Lions football. The Thanksgiving game is a Lions tradition, dating back to 1934, and it is as beloved by fans as cranberry sauce and pumpkin pie. The love continues, even though the Lions have served up a lot of turkeys themselves over the years; they have a nearly even 33–32–2 record and have lost five of their last seven "Turkey Day" match-ups.

DID YOU KNOW?

Soul singer Marvin Gaye once tried out for the Detroit Lions. Being a Detroit Lion was a dream he'd had since childhood, so he bulked up and put his singing career on hold to make the 1970 tryouts. He was rejected immediately. Upon returning to the studio soon after his rejection, he recorded his most famous hit, "What's Goin' On?" Two Lions teammates, Mel Farr and Lem Barney, joined him in the studio to provide guest vocals.

Golden Wings

Hockey fans in Detroit were never happier than they were during the "Golden Age" of the Detroit Red Wings, when the team dominated the NHL for over a decade. The Golden Age began in 1947 when the triple threat of Gordie Howe, Sid Abel and Ted Lindsay earned the name "the Production Line" for their ability to score and win. This trio led the team to nearly annual playoff appearances as well as Stanley Cup wins in 1950 and 1952. They also made the record books in 1950 by becoming the number one, two and three scorers in the league. It is the only time in history that the top three scorers have come from a single team.

After the 1952 season, Alex Delvecchio replaced Abel on the Production Line. The Wings continued to dominate with "Production Line II." They made the playoffs each year until 1959 and won the Stanley Cup in both 1954 and 1955. The Wings continued to lead the league into the 1960s, but they would never again dominate as they had during the previous decade.

DID YOU  KNOW?

During the Golden Age, the Red Wings had the first female NHL club president in history, Marguerite Norris, from 1952 to 1955. She inherited the team when her father, team owner James Norris, died. She was also the first woman to have her name engraved on the Stanley Cup.

THE CAR IS BIG HERE

America's Car Capital

Michigan would be a very different place if Henry Ford had not lived here. From his inventions and innovations sprung an entire economy, one that Michigan thrived on through most of the 20th Century. To this day, the state defines itself in part through its connection to the automobile, and its fortunes rise and fall on the strength of that industry.

Before Ford

Though Ford is credited with perfecting the modern automobile, he was not the first to make one, nor even the first to make one in Michigan. Gas-powered "road wagons" had been introduced in Europe as early as 1860 and in America as early as 1893.

The Olds Motor Vehicle Company in Lansing, a company founded by Ransom E. Olds in 1897, manufactured America's earliest automobiles. Oldsmobile introduced the Curved Dash Olds in 1901 and built 425 models, making it the first mass-produced gasoline engine car in the world. The Curved Dash was named for the unique shape of the footboard and became the most popular car of the period. All models featured a seatside crank for starting (to prime the engine) and a single cylinder, water-cooled, four horsepower engine that was state-of-the-art for its time.

The Great Henry Ford

Henry Ford (1863–1947) was born in what would later become Dearborn, the city where he established his success. As a child, Ford had a great interest in mechanical things, and as a young man he worked as a steam engine mechanic. Soon he developed a passion for gasoline-powered vehicles and founded the Henry Ford Company (which would become Ford Motor Company) in 1899.

It was not just his vehicles that launched Ford to success; it was the way he manufactured them. Most cars of the time were built individually by a small group of workers. Ford instead hired a large number of mechanics and set them up in the now-common assembly line structure, with each employee employed at a single task, thereby reducing costs and speeding up production. Lower costs meant lower prices, and Ford Model Ts began to sell in large numbers. The manufacturing and marketing of the "Tin Lizzie" served as a model for the industry, and before long, every automobile company was switching to an assembly line structure. Because Ford established his factories in Michigan, other automobile companies also came here, hoping to hire away already-skilled workers. And thus did Michigan become the automobile capital of America.

DID YOU KNOW?

Ford also championed "Fordism," the business philosophy that says every worker should be paid a living wage. Specifically, Ford felt that the people who built his cars should be able to afford one. He paid his workers, and adjusted his car prices, to help further this philosophy.

A Tour of History

It's only fitting that the "Automobile Capital of the World" also has a world-class automobile museum. That facility is the Henry Ford Museum, located near Ford's world headquarters in Dearborn. Visitors to the museum can see more than 100 cars from every era of automobile manufacturing, from the earliest gas-powered Olds all the way up to the newest hybrid cars. The entire collection is placed in historical context, along with road signs, advertisements and other artifacts of automotive history. Some famous cars are also present, such as the limousine that John F. Kennedy was assassinated in.

Besides cars, the museum has dedicated itself to other industrial and transportation subjects. There's an entire collection of locomotives and steam engines, and a tour of the history of flight complete with a life-sized replica of the Wright Brothers' airplane. There are also exhibits on industrial manufacturing, classic furniture and popular culture of the 1950s, '60s, '70s and '80s. Henry Ford, who was an avid collector, acquired many of the objects himself, and the museum's collection has even been dubbed "Henry's Attic."

Partnered with the museum is Greenfield Village, an outdoor walk through American history. The village has nearly 80 historical structures, many acquired by Henry Ford himself, that recreate life in Michigan's history. Among the village's seven historical districts is Thomas Edison's actual Menlo Park, NJ, laboratory, which Henry Ford purchased after Edison's death and moved, piece by piece, to the village.

The Big Show

A state built on cars must have the nation's biggest car show. The North American International Auto Show (NAIAS) began in 1907 as the Detroit Auto Show, a regional event featuring many Detroit-area automakers. Today, the show has grown considerably, with more than 90 exhibits from an international

gathering of automakers all filling Detroit's Cobo Center. Companies use the NAIAS to introduce new vehicles, show off their best concept vehicles and generate positive buzz about their yearly lineups. During the NAIAS Preview Night, things are especially glamorous—it's a black-tie and gown media event that gives guests a first look at the show and also raises money for charity. Getting into the preview night will cost you ($400 in 2007), but it may be worth it to rub elbows with the likes of Bill Clinton, Celine Dion, Kid Rock and Jay Leno.

DID YOU KNOW?

During World War II, the manufacture and sale of passenger cars and trucks was outlawed so that all resources could be turned to the war effort. As a result, no Auto Show was held from 1941 to 1953.

DRIVING MICHIGAN

Highways and Byways

Michigan has 1.162 vehicles per licensed driver, which means there are around eight million vehicles on Michigan roads. Michigan highways take a beating because of it, and Michigan drivers have learned to suffer through a construction season that seems to get longer and longer each year. Michiganders routinely refer to "orange bushes" or "orange hedgerows" because, like all the other plants, orange construction barrels seem to blossom in early spring and stick around until the first snowfall. As one old joke notes, there are really only two seasons in Michigan: winter and construction.

The Big Roads

Traveling north to south in Michigan usually involves some time on Interstate 75, which runs across 396 miles of the state. It enters Michigan south of Detroit and wends north to the Mackinac Bridge, which carries the highway into the U.P. I-75 ends in Sault Ste. Marie, right at the Canadian border.

Heading east to west in Michigan offers more options. In the southern third of the state, there are two major interstates, I-96 and I-94. I-96 is unusual in that it is the only intra-state interstate; it begins in Detroit and ends in Muskegon. I-94 begins in Port Huron, loops through Detroit, and heads west to Lake Michigan, where it loops south to Chicago before heading farther west. Farther north, the east-west trip is completed via a smorgasbord of state highways, depending upon one's destination.

Grand Old Main Street

It should come as no surprise that Michigan, famous for its cars, was also the first place in the world to have a concrete paved road. That road was Woodward Avenue, Detroit's most famous street. The first mile of Woodward was paved with concrete in

1908 as a means of battling ruts, puddles and horse manure. The paving made the street much more automobile friendly. By 1916, all 27 miles of Woodward had been paved, making it Detroit's main thoroughfare for travelers and businesses.

In its glory days, Woodward was lined with mansions, estates, restaurants and high-end shops. Most of that architectural finery is gone now, but Woodward has remained one of Detroit's most important streets. Today it stretches through 11 communities, connecting the northwestern suburbs to the city proper. In addition to serving as a significant commuter route, Woodward hosts special events like the Woodward Dream Cruise and America's Thanksgiving Parade.

Stop!

Detroit police officer William Potts invented the four-way stop light in 1920 as a means to control traffic along Woodward Avenue. The first light was installed at the intersection of Woodward and Fort Street, with a second quickly following at Michigan Avenue and Woodward. A nearby traffic cop operated the lights manually, adjusting the changing lights to the flow of traffic.

The Michigan Left

As you drive through Michigan, be ready for the Michigan Left, a much-maligned surface street design feature that often confuses out-of-state travelers. Simply put, the Michigan Left (also known as a "directional crossover") is a feature of divided highways and boulevards that prevents turning left at a cross street. Instead, the driver is required to pass the cross street, make a u-turn on a median crossover, and then make a right turn down the cross street. If the driver is coming off the cross street, he must also turn right and make the crossover to head left. The design was first placed on Michigan roads by two highway planners, Joseph Hobrla and Joseph Marlow, in the 1960s.

Why put so much effort into a simple left turn? Traffic flow. On crowded streets (like Detroit's Telegraph Road, the first to have Michigan Lefts), left turns slow the flow of traffic. A directional crossover eliminates left turns from the intersection, allowing for faster light changes. It also prevents eager drivers from trying to "cut left" against the flow of traffic and cause accidents. Out-of-staters may despise it, but for Michiganders, the Michigan Left is a smart and appreciated innovation in traffic planning.

TEN GOOD REASONS TO LIVE IN MICHIGAN

10. The History. Michigan is steeped in American history, from copper and the Underground Railroad to automobiles and the UAW. Living in Michigan means sharing in its vibrant past.

9. The Wildlife. The mammals, birds and fish of Michigan are a delight, whether you're interested in hunting them, catching them or merely observing them.

8. The Wheels. Especially around Detroit, Michigan is *all about the cars*. Auto afficianados will find plenty of reasons to love Michigan.

7. The Sports. Michigan's professional teams have won national championships in every sport you'd care to name, and many of our college teams are among the best in the country.

6. The People. Michiganders are a varied and vibrant lot, the perfect compliment to any personality.

5. The Soundtrack. From the Motown Sound to the Material Girl, Michigan music rocks the world. We move to our own beat in musical Michigan.

4. The Water. Never being more than 85 miles from a Great Lake means always having fishing, boating and watersports only a short drive away.

3. The Setting. Michigan is all about getting out and getting about. Whether you prefer the grandeur of a symphony, an afternoon at the ballpark or a lazy day on the beach, Michigan gives you somewhere to be.

2. The Menu. Michigan is a state that likes to eat, and you'll love eating here too. There is enough great local and regional fare to please any palate.

1. The Weather. Whether you prefer sun, snow, wind, rain, sleet or clouds, Michigan will deliver…sometimes all in the same day.

ABOUT THE AUTHOR

Brian Hudson

Brian Hudson was born and raised in "Downriver," a suburban town south of Detroit. He earned both his bachelors and masters degrees in English language and literature from Central Michigan University. Writing is one of his greatest loves, second only to his wife and son. Brian has published several articles and contributed to two other books of state trivia. When he's not writing or busy working as the director of learning support services at Baker College of Auburn Hills, Brian enjoys reading, movies, tabletop games and live theatre. In general, he says he loves a carefree day, a good pizza and a great cup of coffee. He hates censorship, cell phones and the state of politics in America.

ABOUT THE AUTHOR

Andrew Fleming

Andrew Fleming earned his English degree from McGill University and has written for such publications as the *Globe and Mail*, *Adbusters*, *Vice*, *Nerve* and *Snowboarder*. Stints as a whitewater rafting river guide, reporter, actor, airline agent, stagehand and bike courier have all preceded this book. He has written two other books for Blue Bike Books.

ABOUT THE ILLUSTRATOR

Patrick Hénaff

Born in France, Patrick Hénaff is mostly self-taught and is a versatile artist who has explored a variety of media under many different influences. He now uses primarily pen and ink to draw and then processes the images on computer. He is particularly interested in the narrative power of pictures and tries to use them as a way to tell stories, whether he is working on comic pages, posters, illustrations, cartoons or concept art.

ABOUT THE ILLUSTRATOR

Roger Garcia

Roger Garcia lived in El Salvador until he was seven years old when his parents moved him to North America. Because of the language barrier, he had to find a way to communicate with other kids. That's when he discovered the art of tracing. It wasn't long before he mastered this highly skilled technique, and by age 14 he was drawing weekly cartoons for a local weekly. He taught himself to paint and sculpt, and then in high school and college, Roger skipped class to hide in the art room all day in order to further explore his talent.

BLUE BIKE BOOKS

More madcap trivia from Blue Bike Books...

GROSS & DISGUSTING THINGS ABOUT THE HUMAN BODY

The human body may be a wonder of natural engineering, but it can also be pretty gross and bad-smelling. In this fearless little book, find the answers to such profound questions as why are boogers green, why do farts smell and where does belly button lint come from?
Dare to read on!

Softcover • 5.25" X 8.25" • 224 pages
ISBN-10: 1-897278-25-X
ISBN-13: 978-1-897278-25-3
$14.95

Available from your local bookseller
or by contacting the distributor,
Lone Pine Publishing
1-800-518-3541
www.lonepinepublishing.com

**BLUE
BIKE
BOOKS**

More madcap trivia from Blue Bike Books...

BATHROOM BOOK OF CAT TRIVIA

Read more about the most popular pet in North America in this great collection of feline facts. How long have felines existed in North America? How high can a cat jump? What do you call a group of cats? Find the answers to these questions and many more.

Softcover • 5.25" X 8.25" • 224 pages
ISBN-10: 1-897278-26-8
ISBN-13: 978-1-897278-26-0
$14.95